Managers Caught
In The Crunch

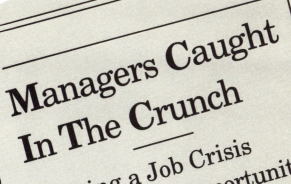

Managers Caught In The Crunch

Turning a Job Crisis
into a Career Opportunity

JAMES M. JENKS and
BRIAN L. P. ZEVNIK

1988   Franklin Watts
New York   Toronto

Library of Congress Cataloging-in-Publication Data
Jenks, James M.
    Managers caught in the crunch: turning a job crisis into a career
opportunity/James M. Jenks and Brian L. P. Zevnik.
        p.   cm.
    ISBN 0-531-15531-5
    1. Career changes—United States. 2. Middle managers—United
States—Dismissal of. 3. Middle managers—United States—Vocational
guidance. 4. Job hunting—United States.   I. Zevnik, Brian.
II. Title.
HF5382.5.U5J44 1988
658.4'09—dc 19   87-34074   CIP

Table of Contents

Preface

The 1980s have confronted many millions of middle managers, specifically a whole generation of individuals in their forties and fifties, with totally unforeseen job crises. Sudden winds of change have blown them far off course from their customary line and staff duties. Overnight they have had to face up to the totally unexpected nightmare of unemployment.

For the first time, mid-level managers have become the central target of company cost-cutters. Under the guise of improving corporate productivity and effectiveness, those bottom-liners have raked scythes through the ranks of middle managers.

The biggest gouges in management manpower have been carved out by some of the bluest of the blue-chip members of the *Fortune* 500. Large companies have followed each other like sheep over the edge of the cliff as the chopped head count of companies continued.

Top executives seemingly spent little time agonizing over how such slash-and-burn techniques would affect the future abilities of their companies to stoke up new heads of steam. Normally, in past cost-cutting flurries, they had left managerial ranks virtually intact, retaining well-trained cadres. Their companies would then be prepared to forge ahead when they had recovered from the conditions which had temporarily derailed them. Not so, this time.

Managers Caught in the Crunch was written to demonstrate that whether you've suffered the indignity of discharge through no fault of your own or are one of the managers still in harm's way, you need not concede defeat. Countless individuals like yourself have learned that while they *are not* responsible for what has happened to them, they *are* responsible for how they respond. They have emerged stronger, happier, and richer (by many measures) than ever before. By learning from their experiences and following their strategies, your life, too, can be refilled with joy and satisfaction.

You will find here—in addition to useful methods to insure yourself against the disaster of dismissal—practical guidance on coping, routes out of your plight, inspiration to keep moving ahead, and hope for a brighter future. You'll see, through the example and advice of others, that there is only one life to live and it's worth living to its fullest. Despite whatever dark career clouds you may be stuck under now, you can fully expect the sun of a more rewarding future position to burst out any minute. Get ready to enjoy it.

Managers Caught
In The Crunch

CHAPTER 1

The Ravaged Ranks of Middle Managers

Caught Between a Rock and a Hard Place

IT felt like getting kicked in the groin." That's how Jack Kable describes his reaction to the devastating news that he no longer had a job at the huge multinational corporation to which he'd devoted seventeen constructive, often exciting years of his life. It was his first real job, other than a couple of years spent in Germany as a lieutenant in the Army to fulfill his ROTC commitment.

"No matter how much people tell you it wasn't you or your performance, it's painful," he says. "It doesn't make any difference how it's handled. You feel rejected, separated from friends. It's not just a job, it's like a family. Your self-esteem is destroyed. You're facing financial ruin."

Jack Kable (not his real name, but his all-too-real story), in the jargon of the professional executive-recruiting consultants, "looks like a stem winder; can make things happen." Even at age forty-two, Jack—at six feet two, 190 pounds—could pass for an all-pro NFL wide receiver. While no physical fitness nut, he does believe in staying in shape by running four miles daily carrying five-pound weights.

And, the results that he achieved during his tenure with a *Fortune* 100 company, as well as at one of its billion-dollar divisions, both for himself and for the corporations, were all-star caliber. So exceptional were his accomplishments that the only people who were as shocked as Jack by his dismissal were his peers, both inside and outside the company.

3

Jack joined the firm straight out of a two-year MBA program—recruited right off the campus. His university's business school, Columbia, has been recognized by everyone for whom such status is meaningful as ranking right up there with the Harvards, Stanfords, and Whartons. That means it's not only among the best in the United States, but in the whole world. For, while the United States may not dominate in every academic discipline, or every art, science, business, or sport, it stands second to none in the formal teaching of business administration and management. Jack's undergraduate degree also came from an Ivy League school. He'd had the best formal business education that could be obtained—anywhere.

A DAY THAT WILL LIVE IN PERSONAL INFAMY

When Jack reported to work one cold Friday morning in January 1986, he had no inkling that before the day was out his psyche would suffer one of the most crushing blows it would ever, could ever, endure. In fact, as the number-three man in a healthy, forward-moving, and profitable division, even more profitable than its parent, Jack's spirits were high, as was his enthusiasm for his personal future and that of his company. He had just completed a fruitful, interesting year—one full of accomplishment for himself as well as for his division.

He'd recently returned from a lengthy trip to Europe during which he'd been a major player in the sale to local interests of one of his division's foreign affiliates. Sure, it had crossed his mind that divesting the affiliate diminished the overall size of the company. It was a profitable move, a wise decision that was in line with the "streamlining" that the parent corporation had already begun in order to concentrate more fully on its core business. The strategy that made good sense for Jack's division, but it cost him dearly.

Moreover, he'd also been engaged, a short time before his trip to Europe, in the acquisition of a company on the other side of the globe. That had turned out very well, too, and was a logical extension of the company's objectives. As an individual who was recognizably racing on the "fast track" in a multinational company, the experiences abroad in acquisition and divestiture, as well as his proximity to operations in the division Stateside, gave a major boost to rounding out his knowledge and skills as preparation for greater responsibility when such an opportunity came knocking.

That it might not be opportunity that was headed in his direction was a thought that had never entered Jack's mind. He'd spent nearly twelve years of his career at the parent corporation itself, and was well known for certain tasks he'd successfully undertaken while there. What's more, his progress from job to job within the corporation at approximately two-year intervals met the customary rotational progress that was well known to be a part of the corporate-culture game plan for fast-rising executives. He had, indeed, proven that he could "make things happen." Just a year before, one of the senior executives at corporate headquarters had told Jack that he was looking for an opening for him there.

Security? That's often been touted as "an old man's word." But it's not something that any person with a wife, two preteen children, a suburban home, and a summer cottage by the sea would brush cavalierly aside. Like most persons with a salary plus bonus nearly bumping the six-figure bracket, Jack was going through the acquisitive years. In his upper-middle-management slot, Jack could afford his lifestyle, and was by almost every measure an outstanding success. He liked his life, his family liked it, his parents were enormously proud of his accomplishments, and he had every reason to believe that his career was poised on a springboard. He did feel secure. He could, should, and did think that his next leap would be upward to catch onto the next rung of the corporate ladder.

HIGH ROAD BECOMES HIGH DIVE

Alas, the springboard cracked. And it was into an empty pool that Jack landed, to join tens of thousands of other middle managers who had also suffered the cruelties of abrupt dismissal and now were struggling to cope with unemployment. Like the others without jobs, as Samuel Johnson wrote, Jack had lost "the safe and general antidote against sorrow." Joblessness was to be his fate for an awful, though mercifully brief, period of time.

A relatively recent change in corporate attitudes has meant that well-paid middle managers—once nearly totally insulated from layoffs—are now subject to the practice of being chopped off just as quickly as hourly workers. The causes of this change in attitudes, as well as its effects on individuals, companies, and the country, are the subjects of subsequent chapters. And so, too, are the remedies and the routes out for those who have been caught in this fiercely blazing firestorm. But for now, back to Jack Kable's thundering "welcome" at the office on that dreary, blustery, January morning: a Friday.

Jack's phone rang, and it was a request from his boss to come to his office. Since Jack had only that week returned from a two-week vacation—he'd been so busy during 1985 that he'd taken no time off—and because he'd wrapped up the sale of the affiliated company in Europe just prior to vacation, the summons wasn't unexpected. No alarm bells rang in his head as he strode down the carpeted corridor toward the executive's suite.

No premonitions. If anything, Jack says, he thought that maybe his boss wanted to learn a few more details about his trip abroad. Just routine.

So he settled himself comfortably in an overstuffed easy chair while his boss shuffled a few papers nervously across his desk. The shocking news was like the Japanese attack on Pearl Harbor—out of the blue.

"As you know, Jack, your position is going to be eliminated" were the very first words his boss spoke. In hindsight, Jack says, he had at least an inkling that would happen at some time. After all, the corporation was shrinking back to its main business. That was an objective, part of its overall strategic plan. Though the corporation, unlike some other giants like AT&T, USX, and Exxon, kept a very low profile about personnel cutbacks, he knew that some heads had already rolled, others were exiting through early retirement, and still others were nervously looking over their shoulders and flashing out the occasional résumé when a likely looking ad appeared in *The Wall Street Journal*.

Then came the real stunner: "And by the way, there's no job for you at corporate headquarters." Jack's mind flashed back to the promise a very senior executive had made to him nearly a year earlier, to bring him back to headquarters.

"He wants you to go over there to see him," Jack's boss continued, "but he called me to say he had nothing for you."

It was a bombshell. Jack knew that the trimming-back could affect his department and might even affect him. That's why just hearing "your position is going to be eliminated" didn't really throw him for a loop right off the reel. But he had been counting on that promise to bring him back to headquarters should push come to shove. But it was too late. The push had propelled him right out onto the sidewalk.

Sure, Jack says, he was given more soothing words

about employee relations looking elsewhere in the company and in its divisions for another job for him. But, Jack admits, "I knew I was gone." And he was.

WHAT'S GOING ON HERE?

Jack Kable's experience in getting the ax may be unique to him. In a way all such separations are. Yet very similar dismissals have been occurring with dismaying frequency all over the country in companies of every size, shape, and ownership configuration.

Sometimes they are done quietly, one on one, as Jack's was. Some large companies send a blizzard of pink slips all at one time—along with an upbeat press release to the media to help prop up their stock prices. An article in *The Wall Street Journal,* Jack says, revealed that his former company had let some 10,000 people go during the twelve months on each side of his discharge. But the reductions in force were being done quietly in his company, as Jack had learned the hard way.

He was—and is—far from alone in his predicament. And later, curiously, that actuality of large-scale mid-management layoffs would become an important factor in his personal fight for survival. It would also play a special supporting role in speeding his comeback.

What is consequential for you, if you're among the individuals who populate these ranks, is to know what's happening, why, and the underlying causes. It isn't that you and other middle managers are threatened with total extinction. It's just that if you're a member of this group, you'll be better able to insure that the wicked fall that Jack Kable took doesn't happen to you. And, in the unlucky event that it does, or already has, being knowledgeable about the current status of middle managers will better enable you to cope with the disaster, climb out of the sinkhole of unemployment, and combat the severe psychological stresses on yourself and your family that such an event causes.

The first step in preparing for potential calamity is to know what's going on in the real world. It's when you're in the dark that fear strikes its most awesome blows. When you turn on the lights and open your mind's door to the realities of your business environment, your fears may not dissipate entirely, but they diminish.

So, you need a crystal-clear picture, at the very least a fast-developing snapshot, of what businesses are doing and have done to thin their managerial ranks. You also need to know the causes of cutbacks, the underlying ones as well as those announced in headlines. For preservation and protection of yourself, you need to look at the effects of mid-management disemployment on individuals, corporations, and on the American economy.

And, difficult as it may seem if you're facing discharge, by knowing what's going on in business, you can be more assured of a happy outcome than those who have preceded you. You can, as have thousands of other threatened and displaced managers before you, live on the old saying, "Problems are simply opportunities in disguise." That's not just a time-worn cliché, as you'll discover from reading later about the successful experiences of others—including Jack Kable. But just as you have no chance whatever of coming out on top in a tennis match or even a volleyball game without knowing whose serve it is, you can't possibly win in the world of business unless you know the score.

WRITE THERE IN BLACK AND WHITE

The New York Times: "AT&T WILL CUT 8.5% OF STAFF . . . 10,900 of the jobs it will eliminate are management positions."

Business Week: "BRACING YOURSELF FOR THE

GOLDEN BOOT . . . In the past two years more than a million white collar workers in some 300 large companies—including Kodak, Exxon, and even IBM have been offered incentives to quit."

The Wall Street Journal: "MIDDLE MANAGERS FACE JOB SQUEEZE . . . Ford Motor Co., for instance, plans to keep reducing its salaried staff right through the 1980's at a rate of about 5% a year."

Letter to AT&T shareholders from the chairman of the board: "Concurrently we are continuing a vigorous cost-reduction program, one aspect of which is a unit-by-unit review of the size of our management force." And in his next quarterly letter to shareholders, the chairman wrote, "About $1 billion of these costs are related to reducing our workforce by some 27,000 jobs, including both management and non-management positions."

From a letter from the chairman of the board of Exxon Corporation: "Dear Fellow Employee: Recent announcements by the company include . . . a major restructuring of regional and corporate headquarters. . . . The necessary reductions will extend to all ranks of executive, management, professional, technical and support staff."

The chairman of the board of General Motors Corporation, its sales of over $100 billion a year making it the largest company in the U.S. in 1986, chipped in by sending a four-page letter in early 1987 to the company's more than one million shareholders. Designed, for all intents and purposes, to encourage them to believe that the company was making all the right moves, it included the following disaster alert (at least to other than Wall Street analysts) which must have sent shivers down the spines of most of its managers: "GM's worldwide salaried employment will be reduced . . . by 25,000 employees in 1987 and by an additional 15,000 employees by the end of 1988."

MIDDLE MANAGERS—
JUST ANOTHER STATISTIC

How many individuals are there who are now very much in danger of getting guillotined? And who are these endangered individuals who, for a multitude of reasons which the next chapter will critically examine, are being given the gate by so many major employers? And what about the ripples these actions cause among the many satellite companies which feed on the business of the giants?

Many statistics have been bandied about. Their sources range all the way from organizations and people who have vested interests in making the numbers very high (or alternatively very low) to the U.S. Department of Labor's Bureau of Labor Statistics. The latter, presumably, has no political ax to grind in publishing its estimates. Of course, as England's most famous before-the-turn-of-the-century prime minister Benjamin Disraeli often said, "There are three kinds of lies: lies, damned lies, and statistics." So, it is with that caution in mind that the following numbers are given.

The deputy secretary of the Treasury tossed out these figures: Between 1983 and 1987, 600,000 to 1.2 million middle- and upper-level executives with annual salaries of $40,000 or more lost their jobs. The next two years, he continued, will see an additional 200,000 to 300,000 similarly situated executives accept the corporate equivalent for career persons of drinking a deadly potion of hemlock.

Fortune magazine takes a somewhat more conservative view. It guesstimated that since 1982, a turning-point year before which the positions of managers were considered almost sacrosanct, about a half million "able and seasoned managers have been jettisoned from the payrolls—and the future of American corporations."

An executive recruiting firm estimates that 35 percent of all middle management jobs have been wiped out
since 1981. The firm did not give a number to which to
apply the 35 percent (hence it will remain unnamed).
But in truth, 35 percent of any number is a substantial
wipe-out. You can see one of the problems with statistics—which will get even murkier when you consider the
next revelation.

The Bureau of Labor Statistics has quite naturally
taken a macro approach to labor-force changes. It charts
by age group "labor force participation rates." It has found
in the age group for men between ages forty-five and
sixty-four (the group to which the great majority, though
not all, middle managers belong) that the percent change
between 1965 and 1986 was *minus* 25.4 percent. Trans-
lation: of people who were employed or were looking for
work, 25.4 percent fewer were actually working in 1986
than in 1965. This rate of change indicates that something quite radical has happened in the business world.
Something has put people in greater jeopardy of losing
their jobs—people who never had to fear receiving that
crushing blow before.

The bottom line is that the number of middle managers has undergone a radical downswing, one that shows
every sign of continuing. The outlook, at least right now
if you're a middle manager earning between $35,000 and
$100,000 a year, is ominous. More and more companies
are climbing onto the bandwagon of reducing the fat, as
they call it, in their bureaucracies, eliminating layers of
management altogether, flattening the traditional corporate pyramid, and broadening the span of control of
the individual manager. By whatever name, they are
giving one manager more persons to supervise and fewer
supporting staff to help him or her with the job.

PROFILE OF THE PEOPLE IN PERIL

When was the last time you picked up your daily newspaper without seeing one article or more about another
big layoff, plant closing, corporate merger, or other em-
ployment-threatening activity? Surely you would have
had to be living on Mars for the last few years to have
missed all the news stories—not to mention the more in-
depth reporting and analyses of these events in the business press, news weeklies, and trade journals.*

As the letters from the chairmen of AT&T, Exxon,
and GM quoted earlier made clear, no one is exempt from
the planned cutbacks, at least no one below the senior-
executive level. The causes of this unprecedented, nearly
violent upheaval make the people occupying middle-
management positions particularly vulnerable. In truth,
they've often become the primary targets for dismissals.

There may be no more "typical" middle managers
than there are typical doctors, lawyers, merchants, or
Indian chiefs. Yet, so many hundreds of thousands of
them have been affected that it is relatively easy to draw
a rough but ready profile of them. You may want to take
a close look in the mirror to see if you fit.

Most of the group which has been at the very point
of attack for the downsizers, the ones who have taken
what will be looked back on some day as an inordinate
or disproportionate share of the heavy blows, is the generation of people now in their forties and fifties. Consider this group for a moment. They were born between
the mid-1920s and -1940s, an era in which the country

* (Interestingly, despite all the publicity, one of the "riffed"
middle managers interviewed for this book said that most
of the many people he's talked to about the middle-management squeeze were surprised when they got the word of their
own dismissal. Their beliefs might result from the same
psychological factor that allows soldiers to plunge into combat—"I'm not the one who's going to die.")

experienced two traumatic events: the Great Depression and World War II. If these hard times didn't leave their marks directly on this generation, it did leave them on their parents, who passed some of the scars along.

One of the major effects of those events was to reduce the birth rate. So, in numbers, this particular generation is relatively small, especially compared to the one following it—known far and wide, sometimes affectionately and sometimes with scorn, as the "baby-boomers." The advantage of the smallness in this group resulted in, among other things, more rapid advancement into middle-management ranks at a time when the economy of the 1960s was growing rather rapidly.

The primary problem that the current forty-to-sixty-year-old middle-management group now faces, though, is that its members are in the most awkward of ages to become disemployed. The younger segment of the generation is in its acquisitive years. Its members are buying their houses, with the aid of huge mortgages which carry what would in the past have been considered exorbitant interest rates, with their resultant very high monthly payments. They're acquiring cars, big-ticket home furnishings, and facing a future of soaring college tuition costs for their children. Even though they live rather comfortably with debt, they little realize that a small debt produces a debtor; a large one, an enemy. Many terminated mid-managers are confronting this enemy right now.

The upper segment of this generation is equally disadvantaged when it comes to facing unemployment. Never mind the laws against age discrimination. Who wants to hire anyone over fifty? Their homes may be paid for, though with today's blandishments by so-called financial experts, a certain number of them have likely refinanced their homes or taken out equity loans. Unlike their younger brothers, debt may not only be inconvenient; it may be a calamity.

Most of them have been employed by the same company for twenty or more years. Even when they made their last change, it was usually in an era of rapid growth, such as in the sixties, when jobs were much easier to come by. And, they were younger. They're not merely out of practice in seeking new jobs, but as one of them put it, "I was really turned off by the idea. The very thought of looking for a job was enough to keep me awake all night and to make my stomach churn all day."

"THE ORGANIZATION MAN"

This generation was brought up at a time when, as William Whyte described in his best-selling 1950s book, *The Organization Man,* there existed a kind of social contract between employer and employee. It was a kind of loyalty which extended from one to the other and was reciprocated. In exchange for following the guidelines set down by the corporation, company, or organization on behavior, dress, patience, attitude, or moving to another company location, the employees were extended the comfort of, if not lifetime employment in the Japanese style, at least a sense of security that their vital needs would be taken care of.

These individuals did learn to expect to get far more than the traditional gold watch and farewell retirement dinner which was the standard that the generations which preceded theirs got for faithful service. Still, working a full week, getting regular, though often modest, raises in pay and promotions, having friends among co-workers, feeling that the company was part of the family—those were the expectations that most of the persons composing today's forty-to-sixty-year-old middle managers were raised with. They came to believe that such a scheme of things was their right and future outlook.

That this dream, or vision, of their march through business life would be shattered at any time was virtually unthinkable, unbelievable, even to the most doubting of Thomases among the members of this group. Now that the unthinkable has occurred to such great numbers of them, their experiences provide some insightful lessons for those of you who are suffering the same traumas or may be in the perilous position where the die may be cast for you to become another victim.

Companies have approached in many different ways the tricky task of trimming, or sometimes slashing, managerial head count. One former chief executive officer, Robert W. Lear, who now teaches at Columbia University's Graduate School of Business says, "Firing people is never easy, but it is part of today's CEO's job. Don't duck the responsibility for seeing that it is done as kindly as possible." Many CEOs have tried to follow that sage advice. Others have simply wielded the discharge ax with callous and near total disregard for the punishing effects that are the inevitable result of unexpected, untimely, and forced separations from employment.

Jack Kable, as reported earlier, felt like he'd "been kicked in the groin" when the bad news struck. Another person interviewed for this book said that when his management delivered its verdict that not only he but everyone in his department was being severed, his first thought was: "I was being dumped out at the curb with the garbage."

SCHEMES FOR THINNING THE HERD

Though hiring freezes and normal attrition through retirement may signal early warnings of work-force reductions, they seldom get quite enough belt tightening results to satisfy the planners charged with cutting costs.

Retirement and other exit *incentives* were invented to speed up the process. Polaroid Corporation was one of the first to start the ball rolling in the early eighties. Its separation plan worked so well that more people took advantage of it than the company had planned for. The same result occurred at DuPont. Nearly 12,000 persons accepted, making it embarrassingly successful. Some who left, it's alleged, had to be persuaded to come back. The government-forced divestiture of its operating companies by AT&T in 1984 resulted in an immediate and highly publicized downsizing of its staff through early-retirement incentives.

By being early players in the layoff game, Polaroid and DuPont had the advantage that neither the middle managers who took the incentives to leave, nor their companies, knew that the noose was beginning to tighten everywhere on middle-management ranks. It was not fully apparent that opportunities for lateral or even upward movement to other firms, which could benefit from their skills and provide opportunities for employment, would be vanishing as quickly as snows do in the mountain foothills on a warm spring day.

More typical of early-retirement incentives was the offer made by Xerox to 4,000 senior employees in the fall of 1986. The company first amended its retirement plan, which already allowed retirement of employees when they reached age fifty-five and also had ten years service. The amendment qualified for increased retirement benefits employees who were at least fifty years old by December 31 of that year and had ten years' service. And, those employees who were fifty-five or over would be credited with five additional years of service and age for the calculation of benefits. In addition, individuals who were below age sixty-two would receive supplemental payments until they became sixty-two, when they'd be entitled to Social Security.

Exxon Corporation took a less restricted approach to

achieve what the chairman noted in his letter was to be "a significant reduction in staff." While stating that previous reductions in the size of the work force had been accomplished largely through voluntary retirements and resignations, and expressing the hope that Exxon would be able to do so again, he also wrote that "the nature of the present situation may very well require an involuntary program as well."

Exxon developed a new "Special Employee Separation Program," which was attached to the chairman's letter. It is estimated that the package was sent to more than 40,000 employees worldwide, which included all those located in the United States.

At headquarters in New York City the company titled four programs in the typically dry, noncommital language of human-resource specialists: Managing Personal Transitions in Times of Change; Career Decision Workshop; Retirement Planning for Annuitant-Eligible Employees; and, Benefits Overview for Non-Annuitant-Eligible Employees. Each program description included a carefully worded footnote which read, "Attendance at this workshop will in no way be interpreted as an indication that individuals are interested in leaving Exxon."

In fairness to Exxon, its approach was more "kindly" than many other companies'. In Chapter 5, which deals with separation benefits, you'll find a more detailed description of Exxon's 1986 program, gleaned from documents obtained during research for this book. In addition to generous severance pay (the maximum allowance payable was twice the employee's last annual rate of normal compensation), all individuals who exited under the program were eligible to continue contributory life insurance, and hospital, surgical, medical, and dental assistance coverages, providing the employee was already enrolled in them.

JUST PLAIN FIRED

And then there's the group of middle managers whose boot from employment is not golden at all. Not every company is rich enough, wise enough, generous enough to work out programs of fair allowances supplemented by outplacement services, stress counseling, and other perks and parachutes.

The golden boots have received the greatest publicity. Naturally so, since most have been designed by the denizens of the *Fortune* 500. Most companies would gladly have forgone the negative ink, except for the fact that announcements of cutbacks in employment usually immediately boosted the company's stock prices, as analysts picked apart the news to find out how much the cutbacks might "tease up" earnings.

It's important for your own career to know what's happening to this beleaguered group of individuals—middle managers. You'll benefit from such knowledge in numerous ways. For one thing, it will open your eyes to your personal options and opportunities for the future. You'll begin to plan better financially so that you won't feel, as Jack Kable did, that sudden unemployment means you're "facing financial ruin." You'll learn from the experiences of others to recognize telltale signs that you may be on someone's hit list. You'll be better able to set up prevent defenses to avoid being the target of the "terminators."

Most important of all, certainly for your future, possibly for your family's future, and most likely for your company's and country's future, you'll be better able to play a positive role for everyone's benefit. You can be a strong and moving force, when you couple your own drives with the powers of all your cohorts who have similar status and goals, when you know and understand more than the bare bones of the situation as sketched in this chapter. You need also to know the underlying causes of the thinning of the ranks of middle management. They are complex, but many of them can be changed by those of you who exercise your powers to influence them.

The "whys" of what's happening to mid-management, the many causes of these surprising changes which only recently burst into corporate organizations, are the subjects of the next chapter. By reading it you will begin to lay your own foundation for new, better, more powerful business and management structures that can better withstand the kinds of earthquakes which have crumbled the structures in which you and other middle managers currently reside.

CHAPTER 2

Why It's Crisis Time for Middle Managers

A Situation Beyond Their Control

BEHIND the eight ball.

If there's any more accurate label than that to plaster on the sticky situation in which middle managers find themselves, it hasn't surfaced yet. Consider this ironic and cruel statistic: The general consensus is that something like 98 percent of managers' terminations have nothing to do with their individual competencies.

These massive discharges are related to factors over which the persons concerned have no control whatsoever. These elements range from plain, low-blow company politics, to macroeconomics, to much more esoteric causes, including the singular thrills enjoyed by the new breed of investment-banking gunslingers.

YOU GOTTA HAVE HEART

What is crucial to you, as an individual threatened with being sucked into this deepening drowning pool, is to know not only what's happening but why. Just as you can know that your bathtub tap is leaking but not know that its cause is a worn washer, so can you know that your position and those of many other managers are under siege, but be unaware of many but the most publicized causes. And this is a case where ignorance definitely does not bring bliss. Knowing the causes, the "whys" of these serious threats to your job, is your first order of business to face up successfully to this ugly crisis.

For those individuals who have already grappled with the unpleasantness of the unemployment-compensation line, understanding the causes helps you cope. That's the unanimous opinion of all the people interviewed for this book. It is an early building block that you need to restore your self-confidence, to raise your shredded self-esteem to where it puts you back in control of your life. Manage your future career; do not let your job manage you.

THE FORCES BE AGAINST YOU

Basically there are two major forces which have clobbered middle management. Together they produce psychological effects on human beings as shocking as the physical damage that occurs when tectonic plates suddenly slip, causing an earthquake while a hurricane simultaneously strikes above. The combination of such physical forces multiply the initial extent of the destruction. The psychological damage to people caused by today's forces, though, lasts much, much longer. Happily, you can take many positive steps to hasten the healing. Later chapters provide guidance for rapid recovery with information based on experiences of others and from experts who are focusing their efforts on this field.

The first grouping of these two forces is located primarily in the economic realm. The second group is largely societal—changing human values. While neither of them stands totally alone—one always has some impact on the other—examination of each group separately gives a fuller understanding of what's behind an unprecedented reversal of fortunes for line and staff managers.

"THE REDCOATS ARE COMING"

Paul Revere's famous warning cry on his midnight ride from Charlestown to Lexington in April 1775 has an eerie echo more than two centuries later. It is true that the cast of characters has changed, as has the situation. It's not troops of soldiers that are on the road, but virtual armies of marketers. And, it's no longer just the British, even though they still are one of our major competitors both in the U.S. and in other markets. The bigger threats are rooted in Germany and Japan. And they have been joined by Brazil and Korea on an increasingly larger scale.

A great many senior executives who served in what is usually characterized as "The Big One," meaning World War II, joked, until ten or fifteen years ago, about the topsy-turvy trading with Germany and Japan. Now it's no longer a joking matter. Rising phoenixlike from the ashes created by Allied bombers have come industrial powerhouses to pour out an unending flow of products which are finding a home in the world's biggest homogenous market—the U.S. of A.

Many of those same senior executives had only to look out their windows at their company parking lots (unless they were in Detroit) or view the crowded freeways to see the most visible evidence of trade victories— the swarms of Volkswagen Beetles, and the Toyota Corollas and Nissan (then Datsun) 210's. These victories didn't happen overnight. Toyota, for instance, exported only 700 Toyopets to the U.S. in 1959. The U.S. had the time to compete before the swarm became a deluge, causing the displacement of many thousands of managers as well as workers.

Perhaps it was inevitable that, as foreign imports cracked the dominance of domestic car manufacturing, auto accessories—and aftermarket auto supplies—would soon follow. After all, why ship a car without tires? More to the point, though, companies like Michelin of France— less hampered it is true by the drag of huge investments in plant and equipment (see Firestone) to serve their domestic original equipment manufacturers—stole a march on American industry with steel-belted radials. U.S.

manufacturers were either happy to keep up with the nation's demand for bias plies, or too myopic to see that Michelins, and later Bridgestones, gave twice the mileage at less than twice the cost, were safer, and provided a smoother ride as well.

One result of this tire invasion was that as long ago as 1980, Firestone had to take an ax to its own operations. Payroll, since then, has been slashed, with managers taking their share of the cuts. The company has announced even more plant closings for 1988 and 1989.

What allowed foreign manufacturers of all kinds (color TV technology was pioneered by American industry— what label does your set bear?) to invade U.S. turf with near impunity is not the real focus of this chapter. The invasion is, though, a factor, and an important one, among the many economic forces which have had a devastating effect on reducing mid-managers' employment.

On this score, there's more than enough blame to be shared by our friends abroad, our government, as well as our industrial leaders, many of whom, for whatever reasons, have seemingly been afflicted by a modern-day tunnel vision in their leadership roles.

A funny thing happened on the way to corporate growth through the route of mergers and acquisitions. By no means a new or unusual phenomenon in the U.S., merging has always played a convenient yet contentious role in the American business scene. What has become "funny" in the past few years of the most recent wave of merging and acquiring is the tortured rationale, or lack of rationale, that the merger masters proclaim as their motivators.

There was a time, some twenty years ago, when the magic words for putting together two or more companies was to obtain "synergistic effects." You seldom read an explanation of the reasons behind combining corporations without running into this favored phrase. Synergy meant, at least to company blenders, that 2 plus 2 adds up to 5. History shows that, more often than not, adding the assets of two companies together frequently produced less than the trumpeted forecast. See, for example, Exxon and Reliance Electric—since divorced. The standing joke among investment bankers and their coteries of lawyers of the sixties was that it was terribly profitable for them to put two disparate companies together. But, they said, where they'd really make the money was from chopping the clumsy giants they'd papered together into multiple subunits, some to be independents, some to be taken over by still other acquirers, and some to be liquidated entirely.

It's clear now that synergy often doesn't occur in the ways about which synergists once publicly brayed. The foremost postmerger and acquisitions thrusts in recent years have been aimed at sweeping cuts in costs. True, in the past, cost reductions were an element in the reasoning. But more important in earlier times was to create greater output and sales, greater competitiveness at home and abroad, and faster growth.

What's even more scary about the latest wave of corporate combinations is that it's almost entirely finance-driven. Whereas in Harold Geneen's heyday of conglomerating equity swaps were in vogue, today's fashion is debt. Merge with or acquire a company, then use its assets to support the debt needed to cement the relationship. The problem, though, is that little of that debt is being used to create new productive plants. Rather, the proceeds are employed to pay off the financiers and investors who merely recycle their take into the next deal.

The debt burden, then, gives management too little time to work out how the newly merged companies can "make beautiful music together." Management must immediately cast an eye on improving cash flow to service interest payments by eliminating jobs and functions. No need for two personnel managers, two advertising departments, two financial, accounting, public relations staffs. One is enough—the other is suddenly redundant, not even given a chance to prove its worth. Pushing aside considerations like fairness, productivity improvements, and synergy, hacking away the relatively well-paid middle managers has become one of the heaviest personnel-related hits caused by the frenzied pace of mergers during the eighties. M&A music has often sounded a sour note.

RAIDERS AND THE LOST ARBS

Boone, Carl, Jimmy—just good ole boys. Are they modern-day Robin Hoods who take riches from stupid, entrenched, senior managers and distribute them to the downtrodden shareholders? That's certainly the way they and their cohorts tell their PR people to portray them in the press.

In an article in *Business Week,* Carl Icahn wrote, "When Mobil and USX had excess cash, did they enrich the shareholders? Of course not." He went on to chastise those managements for making disastrous diversification investments to the detriment of shareholders.

But, as politicians are fond of saying, let's look at the record. Icahn made an unsolicited offer for 100-year-old Dan River Mills. After a bitter fight in which the main opposition became the employees of the company, with their stock ownership plan, he sold out for an $8 million profit. That profit was financed first by burdensome borrowing, then by chopping 2,000 jobs. That's reverse Robin Hood, and certainly didn't make for a bunch of merry men and women at Dan River.

Then there's T. Boone Pickens, Jr. As one of the eighties' most visible raiders, he chased Phillips Petroleum and then Unocal so hard that both companies are now laden with interest on loans. Phillips has knocked thousands of people from the payroll. Boone won for himself millions of dollars of what financial journalists call "greenmail," leaving the "beneficiaries" of his attacks restructured, broke, and unemployed.

Jimmy, Sir James Goldsmith, reached across the Atlantic to make a grab at Goodyear Tire & Rubber Company. Robert Mercer, Goodyear's CEO called him a "greedy corporate raider." His product, Mercer says, is deals. "And that is not a product which a country can make its fortune on." Jimmy's take? A cool $629 million for his shares and $37 million for expenses. Goodyear's fate? Closed plants, laid-off workers, delayed R&D—which further reduces its competitiveness against both domestic and foreign tire makers. Even Black Monday (October 19, 1987) didn't deter Sir James. His heavy cash position left him relatively unscathed and prepared for more raiding.

A BASKETFUL OF CATCH-22'S

Why not simply let the professional raiders take over their targets? It's not that simple. Raiding has become a fine art, to label it nonpejoratively. It's been supported by an unholy alliance of raiders, arbitrageurs, and investment bankers.

The raider picks his target and buys a modest amount of stock. He then delivers an offer to the target company. Lacking the millions (or billions) of dollars that are needed to make the threat a real one, the raider arms himself with a letter from an investment banking firm which asserts that it is "highly confident" that the money can be raised for the hostile takeover. Confident it is, because it has behind its letter not only its own capital and that of certain preferred customers, but also giant pools of money gathered by risk arbitrageurs who've been "capitalized" by a small group of wealthy investors.

These people, unlike you and millions of others with smaller stock, bond, and savings-account holdings, are looking not for just normal "market" rates of return, but rather 30- to 50-percent returns in just a few days, weeks, or months! The arbs jump into the fray, buy shares in the company the raider is assaulting, and tacitly at least, stand ready to support the raider with their acquired shares—later to sell them for a quick profit. Major upsets like the topsy turvy Stock Market last fall? Merely a small blip on their fast-track screen.

Rarely do the wealthy investors, the arbs, or the investment bankers really care if the raider wins his takeover battle. You can easily make a case that they all hope he won't. For if he does succeed, he'll be saddled with a property that at best probably has had a track record of earning less than 10-percent return on its investment. And that's over time—possibly many years, as companies gird themselves for longer-term growth and stability. That's not the kind of action that these people are looking for.

What they are looking for, as noted before, are big-buck gains in very short periods of time. They hope they'll get such returns by forcing, scaring, or manhandling their target companies into buying back the chunks of stock whose purchase they have financed—greenmail, in short. Taxes on short-term gains? Forget it. For that kind of short-term gain, almost anyone would gladly fork over up to half to Uncle Sam—who's now made the tax tariff even less with the tax reform which took place in 1986.

The cozy relationship among the raiders, arbs, and investment bankers became even chummier. As the investment bankers, which typically have their own stock-trading arms, saw the arbs coining tons of cash, they formed or beefed up their risk-arbitrage divisions. Now, under one roof, a Drexel, a Kidder, or a Merrill Lynch could earn commissions by trading for their customers, play the risk-arbitrage game when a likely company target hove into their periscopes (or in their jargon, the company was "put into play"), and underwrite new issues of securities to finance either a takeover by a raider or a defense against one.

To add icing to their cakes, they often charge huge fees for advising the raider on takeover tactics, or for counseling the target company on strategies to resist an unfriendly onslaught. One commercial bank, in fact, has been accused of backing both sides of a contest. While continuing a long-standing, friendly banking arrangement with a client company, it was providing credits, so it is alleged, to a party which was planning a hostile takeover of its client! Another candidate for Ripley's Believe It, Period.

This spider-webbing by members of the unholy alliance has been, for the most part, within the law. Even the questionable morality of engaging in trading, arbitrage, underwriting, and advising by people all employed by the same company is, supposedly, guarded by so-called Chinese Walls. They keep those engaged in one of these activities from exchanging information with others in another division which could profit from it. How porous the Chinese Walls are (the real one didn't keep the Mongols out of China, by the way) came to light when it was revealed that in one Wall Street firm, the head of the risk-arbitrage department was also the head of over-the-counter trading. In another well-known firm, it was alleged that the head of the arbitrage department was called in to advise other members of the firm on their merger activities.

Perhaps the information leaks could have been controlled. Certainly investment companies had controls in place, though most auditors say that collusion will always escape detection for a time. But then the dam broke. It turned out that some of the independent risk arbs were playing with marked decks. Rather than being super-skillful at analysis and picking likely targets for takeovers, they were getting inside information before a takeover offer was made public. In many cases, they were betting on a horse race after they knew the winner.

What does all this mean to you, the middle manager—either unemployed or in danger. This gunslinging has helped shoot holes in many thousands of your jobs, and remains a threat to kill many more. Without letting the follies of senior management completely off the hook for certain ego-inflating decisions, blindness, and arrogance which has caused much chaos in American industry, those executives who played against the dealers with the marked cards, or when "the fix" was in, were whipped before they even climbed into the ring.

Mercer of Goodyear calls such raids "economic terrorism." He avers that raiders, supported by arbs and bankers, force major companies to depart from their long-range plans. Snipers accuse big companies of planning only for better earnings for the next quarter. That's largely nonsense. Some plants take a decade of planning to build before they are up and running. Meantime, getting them into production causes immediate expenses and drains on cash.

But the arbs and bankers are thinking short-term. That puts senior managements at a severe disadvantage. They have to fight the public pronouncements that their companies' breakup or liquidation values are far higher than their stock prices reflect. Raiders make their companies seem to be worth more dead than alive, patently untrue even in the short run. To fight that perception, senior managements resort to massive cost cutting—the quickest being disemployment of—you guessed it!—middle managers. The cost cuts finance buy-back of the raider's stock and their own companies' open-market stock purchases made to increase share prices. It's a zero-sum game; someone gains only because someone else loses.

The raiders, arbs, and investment bankers gain.

Middle managers lose. By one estimate, some $300 billion has been saved by cutting costs, mostly from RIFs (reductions in force). That sum has landed in the pockets of the members of the unholy alliance, who do, it's true, recycle some of it into productive use—like adding a swimming pool or tennis court to the second home in East Hampton or on the Connecticut shore or, to give the West Coast its due, in La Jolla. Small potatoes compared to its scheduled or potential use in more productive corporate pursuits including job creation—or retention.

TECHNOLOGY UNPLUGS MIDDLE MANAGERS

Curiously, considering the numerous introductions of new means of communication, transportation, mechanization, and high-tech inventions over the past 100-plus years, until about a decade ago none of them basically changed the hierarchical form of American management. That form is really modeled on nineteenth-century military organization and the church. The chief executive, managers, supervisors, and workers made up the typical pyramid system.

True, some gradual changes have gone on. While the typical pyramid still had one boss at its peak, and the typical functional production departments also formed little pyramids within the overall organization, some fattening in the middle has appeared. Obviously, as the size of companies grew, new specialists were added for personnel, public relations, research and development, advertising, and legal requirements. And, in addition, more finance and accounting specialists were enlisted for support. Most of these specialists are known as knowledge workers and were, on the military model, staff rather than line.

Then the digital computer burst onto the scene. Little did anyone know that it would ultimately shake to its roots the hierarchical form of organization. Initially the computer created an entirely new set of specialists—highly knowledgeable and well-educated people, who also were placed among support staff rather than directly involved in the production of goods and services.

The mainframe digital computer initially fit quite well into hierarchical managements, albeit creating another small bulge. Quite well, that is, until the microcomputer arrived with a bang in the mid-seventies. Almost overnight any manager who wanted to invest some time and money could have on his or her desk an electronic marvel which could do in minutes or seconds what would take legions of people, or weeks of programming a mini- or mainframe computer, to accomplish. Moreover, having a micro-, or personal, computer on the desk avoided, for the managers who used them, the agony of going through the labyrinth of bureaucratic screening as to needs, priorities, and cost justification. It's no wonder that personal computers multiplied like rabbits.

This dramatically new technology—speeded by advances in communication and easily available, quite sophisticated software—made it possible for machines to perform many *management* chores more cheaply than people, whether they were just workers or managers themselves. For example, no longer did a purchasing department need numerous buyers to monitor inventory levels of various materials or components used in the manufacturing process, determine when it was time for the company to buy, and issue purchase orders for the most economical order quantities. All the above could be done by machine. That not only eliminated many buyers, but it reduced the number of purchasing managers needed to supervise those buyers' activities. While it is true that in large companies mainframe computers had already taken over many of these purchasing management chores, the PC hastened the process in big companies and put the same advantages into the hands of smaller companies. Moreover, in the giant companies, the desktop computers now make it possible for senior purchasing executives to tap into their mainframes for information they want. They no longer need to turn to one or more middle managers in purchasing to get them to compile reports or find a quick item of information. They have it all at their fingertips.

This scenario in purchasing was replicated in many departments in many companies. It's clear that the advances in computer technology have driven whole layers of middle managers into the streets. Computers not only shrank some of the bulge and flattened the pyramid, but also eliminated some functions entirely as companies discovered that it was easier to subcontract them to another firm or to an independent consultant (both choices allowing for a savings on benefits—often estimated at one-third of an employee's salary). More jobs down the tubes.

There's another angle to this impact of computers on the job market. They have not only made many managers redundant as processors of information for senior managers. Computers in the hands of low-level people— individual employees or workers—have also put the squeeze on middle-management ranks. Information that was once created by, filtered through, and passed down by middle managers to supervisors and workers is now directly available through computer terminals to those workers who use it.

This is the downside of the computer revolution. What has actually occurred, though, is a more rapid change in sociotechnical methods than the industrial world has ever seen before. After all, 165 years ago the Luddites in England ran amok to destroy the "automation" of that era in the cloth-weaving industry. Management adjusted. Today, however, the changes that computers spurred in the workplace have been so compressed in time that middle managers aren't being given a chance to adjust—they're just being eliminated, axed, displaced.*

In addition to the economic factors at work, you also need to comprehend the social ones, particularly those which have to do with present-day human values. Unlike the economic elements, which are far removed from your influence, the societal ones, if not within your power to change, are forces which you can adapt to. If adjusting your managing style, for instance, helps you hang on to your job, or encourages you to cope with the crushing blows to your self-esteem, or assists you to nail down a new job during an interview, then knowing the import of social changes is useful. Knowing, understanding, and adjusting to them does not mean compromising your own morals or ethics. Rather, you are able to view the current business and management scene from a more realistic, pragmatic perspective.

LOYALTY—GOING THE WAY OF THE DINOSAUR

"It's not just a job; it's like a family," says Jack Kable when recalling his feelings about having the rug pulled suddenly out from under him.

"There's decreasing loyalty," states Bill Pugh (another alias), former upper-level manager at a giant communications company when reminiscing about missing the brass rings and being fired when the new guy wanted his own players. "The fragile bonds between employer-employee have been broken."

"I'd been transferred several times and always went," comments Roger Schultz, a former public relations man-

---

* There's an upside to the computerization of business and industry, one that means more jobs and opportunities for mid-management people. Chapter 8 will show what these opportunities are for you, how they can give your career a boost, and how you can capitalize on them.

ager at a large engineering- and electrical-equipment manufacturing company. "It used to be when a company asked you to move there was sort of a contract between you and the company. You'd do what they asked and they'd take care of you. That's gone now. Companies no longer have any loyalty to their employees."

More often than not, that is the song being sung by the legions of middle managers caught in the recent RIFs of their companies. And that's a significant point for you and your peers in the forty-to-sixty age group.

If you're like most of the people in that unlucky generation who were interviewed as part of the research for this book, you joined your employer with the idea firmly fixed in your mind that you'd give your job your best and commit yourself to the long-term goals of your company. You'd work hard, protect its assets, receive regular promotions and increases in pay, and stay put.

You'd build up your interest in the thrift plan, participate in the employee stock-purchase plan, brag to your friends and neighbors about your accomplishments and those of your employer. After thirty or forty years you'd move gracefully into retirement with a comfortable pension, regular communiqués from the company about how it and the co-workers you left behind were doing.

Then almost without warning something changed, and corporations' loyalty to their employees went out the window, dragging with it many thousands of astonished middle-level managers. In some cases they were bloodied but unbowed; in other cases, tragically, they left with spirits broken and feelings bitter.

What happened? "There's a new breed of top manager out there," says Roger Schultz. "He thinks, 'The future be damned; it will take care of itself.'" Bill Pugh concurs. "The syndrome of 'me first' was initiated by corporate management. If I, as a manager, know I have security and a career, I can take the long view. If I don't have that security, I can't put the company's interests before mine. That's the new concept being bred in managers today."

The decline in corporate loyalty is particularly poignant because the cost-saving payroll cuts are weighted heavily towards ridding the company of the highest-paid, longest-service employees. The terms to spur departures are generous, of course. But they also rid companies of older managers who are least employable by someone else.

These people have been picked upon for discharge because that's where the greatest immediate cost savings result. DuPont took a $125 million *one-time* charge for its separation program. But it has gained after-tax savings of $230 million *each year*.

ARROGANCE IN THE EXECUTIVE SUITE

The "new breed of top manager" is certainly one cause of the decline of corporate loyalty to employees. Another is arrogance. "When men are most sure and arrogant, they are commonly most mistaken," a philosopher once said. Arrogance adversely affects judgment. In the executive suite it is not entirely new, but is now rooted differently. It was, without much doubt, executive arrogance when Henry Ford the First said, in answer to his managers who advised him to meet the growing competition and to listen to the voices of the marketplace, "They can have a car any color they want as long as it's black." Not long thereafter, General Motors, rammed into high gear by Alfred P. Sloan, Jr., powered past Ford to capture the top spot in auto sales—at one point grabbing more than 55 percent of the U.S. market.

The new breed benefits from what is called corporate democracy. Dutifully they send shareholders proxies to vote. But, in many cases they surround themselves with docile directors. That is their first layer of insulation.

Whenever the heat gets turned up against them, either by raider or Nader, they protect themselves against potential shareholders' wrath with golden parachutes and long-term employment contracts. Ferried around the country in corporate jets, housed in corporate condos or lush permanent hotel suites, catered to by batteries of sycophants, it's not surprising that the new breed has developed arrogant attitudes.

For example, when GM's chairman could no longer stand the carping of a director whose company he had just acquired, he simply bought him off with $700 million of shareholders' money. No, he didn't get stockholders to vote on the proposition. There was no democracy in his action. The distancing of top management from ownership virtually eliminates accountability, and arrogance sets in.

The problem with the executives infected with such arrogance is that it renders them unable to distinguish among the relative values of the mighty three M's—men (women), money, and materials. When a quick fix of the balance sheet is needed, they become blind to the values of the human assets, which are never directly recorded. Unable to see the differences between what people can furnish and what money buys or materials contribute, the arrogant executives dismiss the people.

So, top managers, isolated, secure, and insulated, tell the chosen survivors to chop off some heads. It's a societal problem and an underlying cause of downsizing.

PASSING CULTURES AND
SPEEDING FAST-TRACKERS

Sociologists speak of a nation's culture as the agglomeration of beliefs and traditions which, subject to gradual and continuous modifications, guide its citizens in their behaviors, in the way they live and act. Hence, when you jet away from the U.S. to, say, Japan, you're usually unprepared for the differences between your beliefs and patterns of behavior and those of the Japanese. You experience what is popularly called culture shock, even though your Boeing 747 has transported you from one civilized and industrialized society to another.

Corporations, too, have developed their own cultures. Perhaps the easiest to explain, most celebrated and even long-lived is the culture of IBM. Its founder and chief executive of many years, Thomas J. Watson, Sr., exhorted his troops to take the best of care of the customers, always putting their interests first. Then, he told his senior managers, see that IBM's employees are well treated and fairly paid. He reasoned, and imbued his company with his spirit, that if IBM took excellent care of both its customers and its employees, profits would naturally, nearly automatically, follow and the interests of the shareholders and other investors in the company would be very well served.

These beliefs which Watson instilled throughout IBM have been the guiding articles of faith of the company and its personnel. They have shaped—no, have *become* IBM's corporate culture and have contributed to the achievement of company goals for seventy and more years.

To varying degrees, most companies develop their own individual corporate cultures. More than any other time in the past, though, corporate cultures are being buffeted by current events. And not so subtle changes in corporate behaviors are playing an important role in causing the crisis in which managers now find themselves.

The declining loyalty of corporations to their employees is part of the change in internal and community-wide business cultures. Like a snowball picking up size as it rolls downhill, so are the culture changes gaining momentum. And worse, because they are a cause of thinning the middle-management ranks, they are creating a discontinuity with the past which has grave consequences for the future. Tradition links the future with the past. Wipe out the traditions of work carried by middle managers, and the linkage which provides stability to operations vanishes.

Presently being inculcated into upcoming managers, as well as the survivors in mid-management, is the attitude, "You can't trust top management." Employees at all levels are peering over their shoulders, fearful of spotting the typical trio of head cutters—one employee-relations guy, one boss, and one colleague—marching down the hall armed with sheaves of pink slips. This distrust diverts managers from thinking about the welfare of their present employers as they keep busy planning for the next job. These mid-level manager attitudes, as well as those emanating from the top, are causing less productive corporate cultures. Increasingly, managers are focusing on the short-term. Why should they plan for tomorrow when they may no longer be there?

During the 1970s, the talk among students in business schools and elsewhere was all about the new approach to forging ahead in business. That route was job hopping. Spend a couple or three years here, and a couple or three years there, then jump to the next job—at, of course, a 20- to 30-percent increase in pay. Benefiting from the long and rapid business expansion of the sixties, unscarred (and unscared) by either first- or second-hand memories of the Great Depression, brainwashed by TV's elegant portrayal of instant gratifications of desires ranging from Porsches to trips to paradise, they pushed, and jumped, and hopped.

Moreover, these fast-track kids came from huge numbers of well-educated individuals in their twenties and thirties, some 56 million of them—the baby-boomers. Their upper tier became known as Yuppies—young, urban professionals. They created an inevitable power struggle with the generation they first needed to penetrate or drive aside—men and women in their forties and fifties, the middle managers. And their success has been another cause of the displacements, outplacements, and dismissals among those in this unfortunate group.

Security is not as important for the baby-boomers as it is for their managers. Their skills are greater than any previous group and more in demand. They could, and do, and did, make good on their boasts of job hopping. And when they landed in their new jobs, they wanted their own, handpicked teammates. They hired other baby-boomers, and shoved still more older managers out the door. They didn't "dig" the old corporate cultures; they dug their graves. They've become a driving force in creating new cultures, to the further deterioration of the positions of incumbent middle managers.

To be sure, there are other contributors to the creation of these crisis times for middle managers. Women taking more places in the work force immediately comes to mind. They're creating their own powers of displacement. So, too, are the minorities, not only those who have been in the U.S. for generations, but also the floods of immigrants from the rest of the world.

Careful reading of the major economic and social forces covered here should give you new appreciations of the causes of the near cataclysm which may have violently affected you personally. Knowing why you're affected gives you a leg up on those who don't. Such knowledge creates the foundation on which you can rebuild, not just hope but actual achievement as well. More than rays of hope, there is truly a light at the end of the tunnel—and that light is not the headlamp of an onrushing locomotive. It is the light of opportunity beckoning.

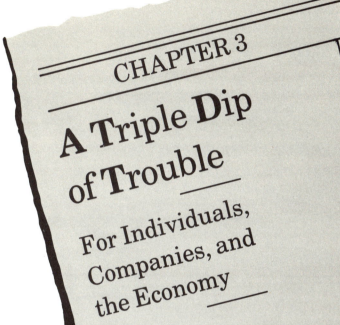

CHAPTER 3

A Triple Dip of Trouble

For Individuals,
Companies, and
the Economy

BLIND-SIDED.

Just as a pro quarterback gets unceremoniously dumped when his head is turned to spot his receiver, so do most managers get sacked when they're not really looking for it. It's not that they didn't feel or see that something was happening to their companies. It's just that they are, with few exceptions, surprised and don't know which way to turn when they are cut down.

That's why it's necessary and helpful for you to consider today the effects of downsizings and restructurings on the individuals like yourself who are affected—the stresses and strains on their relationships. It is also important for you to get a perspective on the effects on companies, their short- and long-term operating capabilities as well as the effects on the economy. This information helps discharged managers, those remaining on the job, and you in planning for personal business futures.

Among middle managers, both the most well-informed business-press readers and the headline skimmers of *The Wall Street Journal* are violently shaken and astonished at their dismissals. Invariably they believed that senior management needed to retain them for their particular, individual skills and difficult-to-equal services.

It's no wonder, then, that their reactions parallel, on only a slightly different level, those which strike persons when faced with what experts consider the most stressful of events, the death of a spouse. First there's shock, then disbelief, grief, and anger, and finally acceptance. So closely allied in its effects is loss of employment to the passing away of a close relative that International Harvester (now Navistar International Corporation), when selling off a division, modeled its outplacement handbook for redundant employees on a book dealing with the demise of a family member.

MANAGERS UNDER THE GUN OF STRESS

Stress is an inescapable fact of life for everyone; there are no exceptions. Stress takes more than one form, exerts more than one effect. It can be pleasant, useful, and stimulating in some instances. You can get a real charge out of stress when you put the pedal to the metal to zoom your car past a slower one on a two-lane highway. Engage in any stressful activity too often, day in and day out, and the stress you feel can quite easily turn into distress, with far-reaching consequences including damage to health of body and mind.

In the business environment in which you spend forty to eighty hours a week in the fast lane, the minor disruptions in daily duties—sudden telephone summonses from your boss, letters or telexes from complaining customers, annoying interpersonal problems dumped in your lap—may cause no more than cold hands as your blood vessels constrict. You can adjust to and absorb such stresses. You may even feel challenged by them. But, according to Drs. Thomas R. Holmes and Richard H. Rahe, psychiatrists at the University of Washington Medical School, a series of stressful events builds up pressures that can become detrimental to your health. Their accumulation over a year substantially increases your chances of incurring some form of illness. Conditions such as ulcers, high blood pressure, headaches, and insomnia are causally related to stress, or more accurately, to distress.

Jack Kable's physical and physiological reactions to the blunt announcement that his job had been eliminated are enlightening and frightening. Before he'd gone to his office on the day he got the grim news, he'd completed with ease one of his usual four-mile runs. That night, he couldn't sleep. Nor could he the next night. Sunday morning he decided that the customary run would help clear the turmoil from his mind. To his surprise and dismay, he found he couldn't finish a single mile. When he stepped on the scale after his shower at home, he discovered that he'd dropped fourteen pounds in less than forty-eight hours! He went for a physical and checked out okay. His sudden weight loss was explained by his metabolism being completely out of whack; his insomnia was debited to worry—and, of course, both were induced by the extremes of stress imposed by his being fired.

Another effect of stress is the feeling of rejection. Even among managers who were dumped along with hundreds of others in a company-wide layoff, the feeling of rejection surfaces commonly and quickly. They did, after all, consider themselves a part of the company family. And now, for whatever reasons, the family has abruptly tossed them out into the cold. Hard on the heels of rejection comes depression. For most people this kind of depression is short-lived. But the down-in-the dumps state of mind can linger and temporarily disable their abilities to act.

RELATIONSHIPS STRETCHED TO THE BREAKING POINT

Strong support for discharged individuals is crucial, especially in the early stages of unemployment. The broader and deeper that support is, the sooner the individuals are able to get themselves together, to begin turning around their attitudes, and to get started on mortaring together the building blocks for their new lives outside of the corporations to which they've been "married" for so many years.

Certainly the separation benefits extended by many large corporations—the ones which have been most "kindly," to use the word of advice of the former CEO quoted in Chapter 1—have been helpful in cushioning the damaging blows. And so has the practical and psychological support rendered by specialized outplacement firms retained for this purpose. (Chapter 10 describes their useful and skillful services.)

But, in the words of Jack Kable: "My firing was handled as well as it could be. But that doesn't matter. It's painful no matter how it's handled. There's no way that good handling can alleviate those feelings of rejection, loss, and humiliation." If you feel that way, that's normal. You'll shake it off when you finally realize that getting fired was not your fault.

There are strains on marital relationships. Strong marriages are strengthened even more. Some weak ones are torn apart, while others are sometimes renewed by the mutual needs for support of each partner. One fired manager didn't tell his seventeen-year-old son about his discharge for six months, for fear he'd worry about his college education. That was a mistake. Most children are more adaptable to change than their parents give them credit for. They often welcome seeing more of you when you're between jobs, and both you and they gain from supporting each other.

Friends and neighbors, oddly, often unintentionally hurt dismissed managers. They feel uncomfortable speaking with you after you've lost your job—another indication of the central role that the corporation plays in all kinds of relationships. How often, for instance, in a social gathering have friends asked you, "How's business?" Now, they don't know whether to discuss the subject of your unemployment or what to say.

What is important for the future of those relationships, though, and for their early return to their former status, from which you can derive support, is that your reactions be within your control. You can *manage* the reactions of your friends and neighbors—you'll be shown how later. And when you learn how to manage your relationships, you'll hasten your emotional recovery and lessen the time for finding your new job or for charting a new direction in your career.

Former colleagues remaining with the company frequently fall into a common pit—fear. It's almost as if you, the dismissed manager, are carrying some sort of contagious disease that they might catch. Your separation from the company, breaking the bond that you once had, makes many of them tongue-tied. And it is true that many of your relationships within the company are based solely on common goals, problems, successes, and defeats. Since you're no longer sharing these, you'll find that some of your former co-workers and you have little, if anything, to talk about.

An outplacement counselor in Westwood, Massachusetts, affiliated with Costello Erdlen & Company, tells the story of a surplused executive who received termination perquisites including an office, phone, secretarial services, and eating privileges in the executive dining room. He noticed that managers who formerly joined him at lunch now avoided his table. When they passed him in the hall, they were always too rushed to exchange words on matters as uncomplicated as the point spread on the next Patriots game, or how the Bosox would do next season.

He finally broke this ridiculous but prevalent pattern. Advised by the counselor to take the initiative, the executive approached his former colleagues with the

statement, "I've got a problem and I'd like your advice."
He wasn't asking for a job—he was asking for assistance. The former associates were pleased to be asked
and to give advice, to lend whatever assistance they could.

BACKLASHES AND BACKFIRES

The fearful batterings of their minds, the burdens on
their spouses and family members, the sometimes
standoffish attitudes of friends and neighbors, the prices
paid in health—all these by-products of dismissal inevi-
tably result in backlashes among severed managers. It
may be incorrect to say that attitudes are changed.
Technically, psychologists say, adult attitudes are well
fixed but can be further developed. In almost all discharged managers, some new attitude development takes
place—or, perhaps, latent or suppressed states of mind
bob to the surface.

Some expert observers of the current disturbing
downsizing scene say that certain managers greet no-
tices of discharge with relief. It is impossible, though, to
determine whether that relief stems from the end of the
terrible uncertainty about when the relentless guillotine will fall, or whether some individuals are simply
tired of riding the company merry-go-round and are only
too happy to be spun off. Such feelings are probably only
instant attitudes; no one really enjoys being unemployed.

A more common feeling or frame of mind found in
nearly every discharged manager is bitterness—not mo-
mentary, but lasting. Jack Kable says that he feels bitter about his discharge and about his former employer.
Yet he answered a question about whether he thought
that trimming management was a wise decision by re-
plying, "Yes. It is the right strategy for the company."
And other managers have expressed their approval of

the tactic of cutting staff even when they were hurt themselves. Even when they recognize the correctness of the decision, they are still bitter. Such feelings are, like that of rejection, normal.

At least part of Jack's bitterness stems directly from internal company politics. He had seen some evidences of political activity during his tenure at corporate head-quarters. Some people had been selected for promotion over the heads of others with greater talents because of whom they knew, whom they played up to, whom they hitched their careers to.

These political promotions, while distasteful, had never directly affected him. But now he was an "out-sider" in the division because he'd been assigned to it from the parent. When word came down from corporate heads to trim management fat, the bosses of the division "circled the wagons to protect their own." The managers they selected to keep in the division were those who had started and spent their careers there. Outsiders, like Jack, were the first to be shown the door. The motivations were purely political, not practical. Company politics is a ruthless game.

Bitterness among discharged managers is almost universal. If you share such feelings, they are common and normal. It would be strange if you spent fifteen to thirty-five years at one company, viewed it as your home away from home, shared its goals, felt the warmth of its embrace, and then escaped without a profusion of differ-ing feelings, including bitterness.

For their relationships with the individuals who re-main with their companies, senior managers should heed Samuel Johnson's words: "Depend upon it, Sir, when a man knows he is to be hanged in a fortnight, it concen-trates his mind wonderfully." Already, remaining man-agers are keeping a sharp lookout on their backs. They're looking for "The Turk," the corporate equivalent of the pro-football assistant coach charged with visiting those not making the team to take them to the head coach, playbooks in hand, for the final cut and one-way ticket for the lonely journey home. The minds of many middle managers are concentrating in ways that cannot help corporations achieve their goals.

What's very much in evidence today is the higher levels of cynicism and suspicion among remaining middle managers. Many of those who have professional backgrounds such as engineering, accounting, or law, but who moved into management slots, are now renewing their professional ties. You should do so, too. They will provide you with further support, assistance, and hope.

WHEN THE GOING GETS TOUGH . . .

Loss of control is another arrow of outrageous fortune aimed at the hearts of dismissed managers. If you have lost your job, or are in imminent danger of being caught in the whirlwind round of dismissals, you can't control the problem, though a group of severed managers at GE did try. They banded together, wrote their outside contacts who were important to GE, and persuaded many of the latter to write to the chairman asking that the discharge decision be reversed. "Their letters hit the round file I'm sure," says one of the group. "It was a futile exercise."

While you can't even influence the event, you can control your reactions to it. The first thing you must do is step back and put your discharge into perspective, as terrible, discouraging, and difficult as this is. Hard? Of course. But you didn't make it to your status in the company without putting in long hours, applying a ceaseless lash to your own ambitions to climb the pyramid, and displaying plenty of courage.

Here's a way to look at it: one person's problem is another's opportunity. An officer of Drake Beam Morin

Inc., the largest specialist in the outplacement profession, says, quite frankly, that the enormous societal problems created by managerial dismissals are opportunities for Drake Beam and its clients—which provides its counseling services to 60,000 managers a year!

You can react positively or negatively to crises in your life. The choice is really yours. The individuals who react positively succeed in viewing their problems of unemployment as an opportunity. That's really essential. It requires support, time, effort, and courage.

Because you can't solve the problem of unemployment, at least by turning back the clock, you must manage it. And that's not quite so difficult as it may first appear to you. First of all, bear in mind, always, that you're not alone. There are literally a hundred thousand and more people who are going through what you are— right now, as you read. Because there are so many thousands of other displaced managers sharing the same leaky boat with you, what counts is how *you* react.

Another important concern for you: don't overreact or exaggerate your plight. Some people, perhaps most do immediately, feel that the end of all they've worked for is near. Look at the other side. The mortgage on your home means that you have some equity in it. You've earned severance pay, vacation pay, and unemployment benefits. You've put something aside into savings—the credit union, thrift plan, 401(k) plan, stock purchase plan. You may have profit-sharing money that belongs to you. You can cut your expenses. Financial ruin is not close by. As your minister, priest, rabbi, or parents have often exhorted you, "Count your blessings." Count the intangible ones as well. Make a list of them all. You'll feel better, stronger, and more prepared to rebound faster.

It's an old truism that successful salesmen stand adversity better than most people in other occupations. They get rejected every day. In their battles for sales they lose more often than they win. More importantly, though, the good ones make things happen; they don't just wait for them. Now it's your turn to sell the most precious commodity over which you have total control—yourself. Set your mind on making something happen. You'll read about how to do that with the tested techniques given later in this book.

Keep control of your career in your own hands. Don't surrender it to friends, employment agencies, employment counselors, or others. That doesn't mean you should forgo their help. Use it, but control how they help you. Don't let that control slip into the hands of others, answering the siren call of what looks like an easier way, when that way is full of avoidable detours and delays. Everything that you do keeps you in control, gives you the initiative. That's what you need to restore your enthusiasm, bury your bitterness, and climb up out of the quicksand into which, through no fault of your own, you've been pushed.

THROUGH NO FAULT OF YOUR OWN—keep that thought foremost in your mind. It's as true for you as it has been true for many thousands of others who, sandbagged by job loss, picked themselves up, brushed themselves off, and started all over again—and won.

CUTTING THE GORDIAN KNOT

While in no way can the sufferings of individuals be compared to what happens to entities like corporations, which derive their "lives" only through operation of law, companies are affected by their top managements' sometimes lemminglike movements toward self-destruction or at least permanent disabilities. The decisions taken to solve internal problems by means of restructurings raise questions whose answers may shed light on the routes out of their dilemmas for affected middle-level managers.

Legend has it that whoever untied the knot with which the king of Gordium had fastened a yoke to the pole of his wagon would become the ruler of all Asia. Alexander the Great examined the Gordian knot, then drew his sword and with a single stroke severed it. That was his solution to what appeared to be an insoluble problem.

Are the bosses of business taking a similar stance to the perplexing problems of beating back competitors, the junk-bond raiders, and Wall Street's junior geniuses? Are they taking the quick and dirty way to cut through complicated questions of costs by striking at the most visible and vulnerable one—payroll?

The plain fact is that when top managements announce restructurings they're really admitting "We screwed up." It wasn't you or the other middle managers now cast adrift who laid on new layers of bureaucracy. You didn't make the faulty decisions on expansion through conglomeration. You didn't even hire yourselves. Yet, it is often the same senior executives, creators of the problems, who offer others as sacrificial lambs in payment for their follies.

While in the short run many senior managers escape paying the piper, the companies they lead suffer. These massive knockdowns of middle-manager head counts have both current and future effects on the abilities of corporations to fulfill their missions and even to remain viable entities.

CORPORATIONS PAY THE PRICE

No question: it's already too apparent that the most immediate downside of any downsize comes from its deleterious effects on the morale and productivity of the remaining managers. Not only are they learning firsthand to scrap their former views of the corporate culture from the sight of vacant desks all around (one former GE manager says that GE's Fairfield headquarters looks like it was hit by a neutron bomb: all desks, chairs, and offices—no people). But also they have had hammered home that tenure from now on can't be more than five or ten years, no longer till retirement do them part.

When you're continually bracing yourself for the knock on the door of "The Turk," or the sudden appearance of the guillotine masters who arrive to tell you you're out and read you your rights (benefits), you can't be an effective planner, organizer, controller, or coordinator for the long, or even the short, term. Even though chosen to remain, you've lost a step in your effectiveness as a manager. Moreover, your morale and productivity sag.

Ironically, senior managers are now flashing signals that they recognize these demoralizing effects. They are engaging consultants to come in to "revitalize" the human resources of the company. They're rushing in damage-control parties to plug up the holes before the seas rushing in sink the corporate ship. That's good news. People upstairs are waking up.

The change in corporate loyalty has its flip side: the loss of employee loyalty to employers. These weakened allegiances in past partnerships cast doubt on the promises implied, written, or stated about future opportunities within the company—for promotions, pay increases and personal growth. Have the U.S. chief executives learned nothing from the "invaders," the Japanese? They have the record to prove that loyalty among employees is the key to high productivity. This lesson has not yet, quite obviously, been fully learned.

Some observers claim that the reductions in the size of the work force and the numbers of managers haven't had and will not have any effects on the capabilities of companies to produce. Baloney. Those upticks in stock prices are merely the knee-jerk reactions of investors advised by their friendly financial planners. The plain fact is that you and other displaced managers will be missed.

What about the image of the cut-down companies in the eyes of what surely must be a most important public, their customers? Even individual consumers are frightened when people they know are laid off and resentful enough to boycott buying certain products.

But more important are the large purchasers of equipment, materials, products, and components. They are often radically upset when they perceive or believe that a large supplier has a diminished capacity to deliver. They will at the very least pick alternative sources, place test orders, and make lesser purchases from companies they think will be hampered delivering, if not quantity, then quality. Shrunken companies have lost customer loyalty and with it future sales. One Chevron dealer bemoans the cutbacks: "There's no personal touch anymore." The marketing reps skip in-person calls as fewer of them struggle to cover more accounts.

Then there's the effect on corporations of the voluntary incentive-to-leave programs. Because of the nature of these programs and of the people to whom they're offered, many companies are losing the best and the brightest. Those "B&Bs" jump at the opportunity to take off with a sizable sack of gold to immediate new employment elsewhere.

The less bold, the more cautious, the risk-averse, and especially the older managers cling to what's in their hands—their jobs. For the company, what could be an opportunity to sweep the decks clear of truly redundant and unproductive people actually turns out to be the reverse. Rather than becoming stronger through layoffs, management collectively becomes less able, at least until the "Mr. Nice Guy" approaches of ushering managers out the door are replaced by more selective finger-pointing ones.

Sometimes Even on Sunday

Successful corporations have never been manned by nine-to-fivers. The personnel cuts have exerted far more pressures on every remaining individual in management. For example, an experienced mid-manager of a more thinly manned company now has less time to train and develop subordinates. Over time, less training and mentoring guarantee more errors of omission and commission, with resultant pernicious effects on output as well as productivity.

When Northwest Airlines acquired Republic Airlines, the chairman of Northwest, according to *Business Week,* sent a memorandum to the surviving Republic managers. Its message: Arrive at work before 8 A.M.; don't leave until work is completed; come in at least two Saturdays a month. That's pressure, especially on managers who are already traumatized by the unknowns that come with reporting to new and unfamiliar bosses.

True, the merger made much better sense if the company could get more work done with fewer managers. It remains to be seen what the long-term effects will be on service, sales, and revenues due to the demoralizing of the acquired Republic managers. One fearful specter is burnout, which is becoming increasingly troublesome to companies as stress turns to distress. Burnout causes personnel turnover. It produces heavy costs of hiring and training and also reduced managerial effectiveness until the replacements learn the ropes.

Reducing the number of managers slows opportunities for advancement. Management guru Peter Drucker predicts that many of today's middle managers will occupy the same positions for thirty years. He associates his remark with the changes required in managerial skills due to automation, as well as the difficulties of absorbing the population bulge—the pig in the python—of the baby-boom generation.

Assuming that jogging in place will be accepted with equanimity by managerial types who are worth their salt, these situations erect almost impenetrable roadblocks for supervisors, junior executives, and entry-level individuals. They are already frustrated, they say, by the old-style corporate hierarchies which stifle their creative efforts, decision making, and participation in the enjoyment of running organizations.

The big casino which corporations must draw for? How to recruit young talent when their avenues for advancement are narrowing. How to hold onto those they do bring aboard when the middle is already stuffed and being reduced at the same time. Careful studies of these issues by the still-employed managers alone are enough to cause an exodus of those persons that the corporations least want to lose.

THE SHORT AND THE LONG OF IT

All Wall (as in Street) is divided into three parts: the brokers, the deal makers, and the analysts. The brokers just want to turn over shares. Whatever a company does— right, wrong, long-term or short—is okay with them just so long as it stimulates buying and selling of shares. The deal makers want instant growth in share prices. If companies can't hack that, they'll create it. And then there's the analysts. Their roles being ill defined, they continually claim that managements neglect long-term corporate investments needed to produce steadily increasing profits for the future.

A case in point: Goodyear was pursuing a strategy of growth by acquiring diverse companies which fit into its long-range plans. Acquisitor Goldsmith, citing the breakup values of the components that Goodyear had carefully stitched together, made a tender offer for the company. No one knows, perhaps not even Goldsmith

himself, whether he actually intended to operate Goodyear after takeover. No one knows either whether his
plan to sell off parts of the whole would have maximized
shareholder values.

And there's the rub. Anyone who believes that Goldsmith could have instituted and executed his new plan
quickly and efficiently with as little information as he
had about Goodyear's operations and markets has been
taking the pipe too often. Changing course for a behe-
moth like Goodyear can be accomplished about as easily
as making a fully loaded supertanker turn 180 degrees
in the harbor of the Isle of Wight. There are no advance
guarantees of satisfactory results from such efforts. Radical strategic changes always have the potential for ca-
tastrophe rather than success.

What is now known, though, is that Goodyear's Board
of Directors decided to travel the prudent route by keeping control over the company's future. It did so knowing
that the cost of independence meant partly mortgaging
the company's carefully planned future and that it could
not achieve as rapidly its previously approved corporate
goals. Even at a high cost, the Board believed that its
decision was in the best interests over the long run of
its customers, shareholders, and employees.

So, Goodyear did dive deeply into debt. And that
plunge exacted costs of considerable magnitude, though
less than a breakup by Goldsmith. One cost: a minimum
10-percent cut in the research and development budget.
That slash will reduce international competitiveness. "For
being a virtual role model for the recommendations of
the 1985 President's Commission on Industrial Competitiveness we became vulnerable to a corporate raider,"
says Chairman Mercer. "Such attacks don't enhance
companies' international competitiveness," he contin-
ues.

Cuts in R&D expenditures may not immediately affect corporations. But what about the years down the

yellow brick road? Without the new products which result from R&D, companies live off their established ones. Milking the old products turns the company into a cash cow. But when the "cow" dries up, as they all do, what happens to the company then? More jobs down the drain.

THE POLITICIANS COME TO BAT

One of the least publicized but most dangerous potential effects that top managements are creating by chopping payrolls is the introduction of more restrictive, anti-business, legislation. Most executives look with loathing, and with not a little fear, at government interventions. Government usually steps into the affairs of business with all the insouciance of an elephant stepping into a mudhole, and the whole business world shudders.

The 1980s wave of restructurings and mass layoffs of employees has set off among politicians loud screeches for legislative action. What companies are doing is stirring up vast reservoirs of resentment which are likely to come back to haunt them in the halls of Congress and in state legislatures. The politicians are reacting. They know that the bosses have screwed up. They see that, even when profits decline, the senior managers continue to receive huge six-figure bonuses. When the disemployed are in the supermarkets buying cheaper cuts of meat to stretch their severance pay, their former bosses are still feasting in their private dining rooms.

Leadership means sharing the pain. The failure of many leaders to do so is stirring up anger and ill-will that's focusing legislators' attention, as it has never been focused before, on the issues of sudden and abrupt dismissals, buyouts by raiders, and plant closings. As long ago as 1974, legislation was introduced in Congress that requires advance notice of plant closings, and it has been reintroduced every year. Several states have hurdled the feds inaction to legislate restrictions on management's freedoms. Lest a company keep a plant nominally "open" (with, say, one employee), the new state laws zero in on work-force reductions as their triggers for notifications. Moreover, some states tack mandated severance pay onto plant-closing laws.

ECO 101—PEOPLE POWER THE ECONOMY

Once politicians start imposing requirements for plant closings and severance pay, "social programs" won't be far behind. Parental leave, child care, and permanent postretirement health insurance are only a few of the plethora of other benefits that agile, politically motivated minds have pushed to the fore and floor. What's important for you here is not to argue the justice, fairness, or needs for such benefits.

What is important for you and for top executives to understand clearly is that the farther that governments intrude into private lives and businesses, the more depressing such controls will be on the nation's economy. U.S. business leaders should learn that whatever they do that triggers greater government regulation is going to backfire quickly. Their actions on downsizings not only have microeconomic effects on their own companies, but also, when joined by many other companies, have macroeconomic effects on the state of the nation's economy.

Running businesses still takes people. No matter how much money, raw material, and machines are thrown into the pot, with no people to stir, nothing happens. While the greater effects of the large disinvitations of mid-managers from the corporate tables of organization will not be known for five or more years, unless most senior executives are hopeless Malthusians, they're creating a terrible waste of human resources. Such waste has a price. And that price will be a weaker economy. Everyone then suffers.

Another effect on the economy resulting from re-structurings lies in constructive use of capital. Driven by financial considerations almost entirely, capital is not being put to creative use in marketing, new-product development, modernizing plant and equipment, expansion or job creation. The only winners seem to be the go-betweens and their support troops. These are transfer payments, no more, no less—in the same league so far as economic growth goes as unemployment payments and welfare, without their compassionate justification.

Economic changes from downsizings also appear in this country's manufacturing capacity. It is not true thus far that the U.S. is abandoning manufacturing for a service-only economy. According to the Bureau of Labor Statistics, there has been no appreciable decline in manufacturing employment in the last two decades. What is true, of course, is that the growth in total employment comes from the service sector. And, contrary to the impressions many biased people would like to give, not all those service sector jobs are minimum-wage, hamburger-flipping types.

The real job growth, again according to the Bureau of Labor Statistics, has been in managerial, administrative, and professional positions. Moreover, the loss of jobs in the sunset industries has been offset by businesses that didn't exist a couple of generations ago—a shift from shoes and cigars to industrial instruments and computers. The loss of experienced individuals like you in the managerial work force poses real problems for manufacturers as they grapple with the tricky tasks of transitions.

A most troublesome problem for the economy is the creation of the prematurely jobless. Not only is their productivity and output lost to the economy, but they become a heavy burden on the remaining employed. Despite their experience and skills, some people who are forced into early retirement will never work again. Some over age fifty-five won't even try.

The economy also suffers as the cuts in middle managers reduce companies' abilities to meet and beat foreign competition. The fluctuations in the value of the dollar, especially when it becomes weak against the fiercest foreign competitors—Japan and Germany immediately spring to mind—may temporarily mask competitive weaknesses. History has shown that benefits from changing values of currencies are never permanent and often elusive.

Can the economy survive? Of course it can. It would survive much better and thrive more readily if senior management swung the ax less carelessly among middle managers. Wastes of human resources, misuses of capital, reduced competitiveness, and the burdens of prematurely jobless people all have impacts on the economy. How dire they will be depends upon how quickly top executives learn their lessons.

It's important for you to know and to understand the negative results and negative effects of this entire situation. The most important mission of this chapter, though, is to buttress your feelings of self-worth. You *are* important to yourself, to employers present, past, and future. You are worthy and needed. Your present situation, whether you've actually been displaced or are threatened or have gone through the tempering fires and are now reemployed, came about THROUGH NO FAULT OF YOUR OWN. That's the message you must absorb to enable you to polish your skills to deal with your own personal stakes in the process.

Famed psychiatrist Karl Menninger once said: "Hope is a necessity for a normal life. . . . it implies progress; it is an adventure, a going forward—a confident search for a rewarding life." The rest of this book is devoted to matters that instill hope in you, that give you proven ways to insure your search for a rewarding life. The difficult you can do immediately; the impossible just takes a little longer.

CHAPTER 4

Devising Your Own Prevent Defense

Strategies, Tactics, Techniques

PREVENT, as in making sure the downsizing steam-roller doesn't squash you in its travels. *Prevent,* as in holding the line on your own job—making it less vulnerable to being eliminated. *Prevent,* as in avoiding the trials and tribulations of joining the ranks of unemployed middle managers in the first place.

Is getting sacked inevitable? Notwithstanding the turbulent picture painted for you in the first three chapters, the answer is, of course not. Despite the mass reductions in the ranks of middle managers, for every one let go, two have been retained. For example, one major employer sent out 42,000 letters offering early-retirement incentives to those eligible (or made eligible under its terms) and inducements to others to seek employment elsewhere (or risk later termination without the incentives and benefits). But it also passed the word, albeit circumspectly for legal reasons, that the company would like certain persons to stay.

This chapter deals with the strategies, tactics, and techniques that you can use to keep the guillotine from falling on your neck. That way, you'll be numbered among those individuals who get the message "We really do not want you to take our offer and leave" or even better "despite what is happening to others, you've made yourself too valuable to be let go."

There have been millions of words written and spoken about how to improve everything from your business writing and speaking to your breath at board of directors meetings. In fact, if you plan to try to improve a specific individual skill (like speaking), it will be worth your while to find a good book that covers the topic from A to Z.

The less than a million words in this chapter deal more with the circumstances surrounding an individual placed in the precarious position of having to defend himself or herself against forces beyond individual control. Reductions in force, downsizing, personnel budget cuts can't be stopped. But they can be deflected. By carefully planning your personal professional defenses, and being alert to the warning signs of job-loss danger, you may be able to avoid becoming a member of the target termination audience.

THE MANAGER OF THE FUTURE

While your nose is still kept to the job grindstone, it's in your best interests to keep a weather eye on what's going on around you, both internally and externally. As you keep your fingers on the pulse of what's going on "out there," you're sure to come across some hints as to what tomorrow's manager will be like. So protect yourself by becoming tomorrow's manager today.

A survey of corporate leaders, for instance, focused on what qualities they were looking for *in themselves* for the future. They indicated they would need to be more intuitive, conceptual, long-term oriented and anticipatory. Plus, they saw that they would be required to take more risks. If you're planning to join these ranks of American business leaders, you should check out how you measure up on those qualities.

Entrepreneurship as a management characteristic is becoming increasingly valued, even at old and well-established organizations. New managers are being asked to cultivate attitudes closer to those of pioneers of the past, to create new strategic visions and stimulate old traditions of employee motivation and participation.

How well do you fit this manager of the future? Ask yourself:

- Am I an in-house entrepreneur?
- To what extent do innovation, intuition, anticipation, mark my own management style?
- Have I devised strategies to overcome threats and take advantage of opportunities?
- Do I have a vision, a plan, a strategy for my own area of operations?
- Do I communicate my vision to subordinates and colleagues?
- Do I monitor progress toward fulfillment of that vision?

There are other portents of the future manager that can be gleaned from a close reading of today's tumultuous business arena. You should be doing that "reading" every day. Whether you're leafing through the local newspaper or a national magazine, or even watching television special events or business programs, file away any and all relevant tidbits of information. Look for common or repeated themes. Combine related information you've picked up from news reports, trade articles, even cocktail conversations.

Stay abreast of the news. Monitor ongoing stories in business and trade journals. Check out the headlines. Pool information with colleagues and pump them for insights into trends and implications they see developing. You'll find lots of other "manager of the future" characteristics in your reading. For one, the managers who survive downsizing will be those who tangibly improve a company's products or profits. The day of the "value-added" manager is at hand, whose job is riskier and more demanding, but also more purposeful and rewarding.

For another, future managers will spend more time utilizing their professional skills than dealing with the corporate bureaucracy. They will place less emphasis on writing reports and filling out forms, and more on exercising their special crafts, be it in sales, engineering, marketing, or accounting. This will be good news to GM chairman Roger Smith, whose second fondest wish is reportedly to wean his vast platoons of by-the-book managers away from their dependence on memos, committees, and reports. He's looking for an "intrapreneurial" attitude in his managers, a thawing of what has been labeled the "frozen middle" at GM.

Maybe that's what your company's top dogs are looking for as well. Recognizing this, you should be more willing to get out of the batter's circle and take your cuts. Throw off what psychologists call the "learned helplessness" that occurs when a person is long accustomed to following systems strictly by the numbers. Make some independent moves, take a couple of risks, if that's what your reading of your own situation calls for.

Further, emerging wisdom claims line positions will move ahead of staff in the corporate pecking order, so grab a profit center to control if you can find one. And speaking of profit, contributions to the bottom line will become even more the measure of the successful manager as the ranks of middle managers are thinned. New management cultures will place more emphasis on monitoring a company's routine operations to make sure none are growing fat and unprofitable.

Another personal skill that will assume increasing importance will be negotiation. As the lines of matrix management open up, there are fewer lower-ranking butts to kick and more equal-ranking ears that have to be bent. The job of middle managers will assume more of the attributes of a coach and team coordinator as increasing numbers of players are cut from the squad. The relay of information will be more horizontal with other coaches, than vertical between the front office and the players on the benches.

WHO THEY GONNA CALL—COST-BUSTERS!

Want to really cement your status in your present job? Lower company costs. Cost containment consistently tops the charts when top executives are asked to rate areas of corporate concern. So as you develop your own system for becoming a manager of the future, be on the lookout for potential cutback areas as well as the techniques for implementing your plans.

One way to contribute as a cost-buster is to conduct an activity value analysis. Look at each task that comes under your aegis and determine its contribution to the productivity and positive results of your function. You may uncover some ways to rearrange jobs and systems that will make your part of the overall organization more cost-effective. Once you've found a suspect section, emulate corporate strategy by forming a mini–task force to systematically decide where cuts might be appropriate, when delegation could produce better results, how lower-level employees could be used more effectively, and so forth.

Another way is to set up a corrective-action team aimed at attacking specific problems. Set up a feedback system from your work force because that is often where the best ideas will come from. Then you can *give credit* to your subordinates for their solutions, and *accept credit* for managing such a good system when your superiors see your positive results.

Specific techniques to attack costs are varied, from

putting a price tag on expenses in doing things wrong (cost of quality) to determining what it costs a competitor to do some task or operation (benchmarking).

Perhaps the simplest target to place in your cost-cutting sights is paperwork. Everyone from the top echelon to your fellow middle managers to your subordinates will appreciate a system to cut paperwork. It even has its own name at General Motors—deproliferation. So deproliferate away. Lead the way to less paperwork. Demand that reports be no more than three pages long. Run a kangaroo court for offenders and force them to cut their too lengthy tomes. Get everyone involved in the effort. Target other unnecessary paper-generators, such as regulations and forms. Solicit nominations for the worst and set up a system to eradicate them.

FROM COST-BUSTING TO IMAGE BUILDING

"All managers are looking for the edge these days. And it's not necessarily that you do a better job, but that it appears that you do."

That comment from a manager who suffered the slings and arrows of a RIF may sound cynical. But in many cases, it's all too true. It's not enough anymore that you work hard and let your record speak for itself. Sometimes you have to raise your voice and speak for your record.

Some managers target their "personal public relations" efforts too narrowly. They focus only on those who have power over their job fates. You certainly do want that group to know who you are, what you've done for the company, and what future values you're capable of bringing to the organization.

But you also want your "fame" to spread to other groups—middle managers and supervisors throughout your company, influential community leaders, movers and shakers in the industry, even subordinates whose loyalty to you could be the deciding factor when a management cut is contemplated.

PRACTICING PERSONAL PUBLIC RELATIONS

Take advantage of your company's communication system. That doesn't mean to flood the channels with extraneous material. It does mean that whenever a report, presentation, or informal discussion is called for, you should get in line to report or present or discuss. Plug the efforts and achievements of your team, group, division, task force in company house organs. You'll be seen as a successful leader who passes the medals of honor to the troops.

Use memos as the communication of choice when you want to spread the gospel according to—you. As long as it's not transparently self-serving, you can elicit deserved credit for a good idea or program, expand your intracompany network, impress people with your systematic approach, and even cover your tush if you're in disagreement with another proposal. As noted at the top of this chapter, lots of publication space has been allotted to in-depth discussions of how to write a good memo. It's essential that you use the weapon. It's up to you to learn how to do so effectively.

Two warnings, though, are appropriate regarding memos. Don't start pumping them out like water. Be selective. Use them when they reflect best on your accomplishments. And don't be a "flamer," a person who gets angry and fires off a memo without sitting on it at least overnight for reconsideration. While you're writing, consider a regular contribution to those in-house company publications. They are always looking for material, and a by-lined article or an interview that shows your savvy to advantage can catch the eyes of the powers that be.

Eye-catching dress, on the other hand, can be a negative in your personal PR plan. One study involving managers at companies suffering through mass assassinations found that meticulous dressers were significantly more likely to lose their stripes than their less meticulous brothers (and sisters). Top executives often look askance at resplendent Ken-doll types. Just look at the classifieds for management positions—is there any adjective more in vogue than "shirt-sleeved?"

And while you're considering how to dress, best polish up your social skills too. How you act at client cocktail parties, industry conventions, power breakfasts, and even company picnics, can help make—or break—your career.

You may flinch at the thought, but even that ubiquitous company picnic offers you the opportunity to practice your personal PR. Some managers approach the event just as they would a business meeting. Set a strategy. Lay out a plan of action. Establish a series of do's (do: volunteer for a committee, introduce yourself to senior executives, avoid criticism of individuals and company policies) and don'ts (don't: be overcompetitive, use adult language or humor in front of children, spend a lot of time talking shop). Sounds like a lot of politics, and it is. But your internal PR program must take politics into account. It's a fact of corporate life.

Write and read and speak. Sounds simple, but it's not. One of the best ways to heighten your visibility is to be published. Write an article for a trade magazine on a business subject in which you're expert. Or create an article on a personal topic (hobby, off-hours project), and focus on publications in that field. Or check on hot local topics and send a proposal to an editor. Again, entire sections of bookstores are packed with "how to become published" publications. Check them out.

Read a lot, especially about local matters. Review the editorial pages. Get to know important issues, organizations, individuals. Take a stand or join a group. Offer to speak in public. Pick an appropriate group (businessmen, church, social) and an appropriate topic (for them as well as you) and get behind the microphone. Or take a stab at teaching or lecturing at a community college, business school, professional seminar.

The point is to become more visible, to obtain a higher profile. If you sat down and analyzed your own visibility quotient, how would you answer these questions?

- When was the last time you signed up for a community fund drive?
- Have you recently volunteered to join or lead a local task force?
- What groups have you spoken before in the last year (community, professional society, government, school, trade association)?
- Did you ever lead an issue study group on an important local matter?
- Are you in a position to be quoted for an article in a trade publication or a local media outlet?
- When was the last time you listened to a radio talk show and thought you would have made a better guest?

Your basic aim in any PR campaign is to get others to know you, and to sing your praises for you. Friends, neighbors, colleagues can all become valuable voluntary publicists.

As your personal PR campaign perks along, keep track. No matter how successful it is, it may not save you from the firing squad. But if you are forced to leave, make sure you take anything that reflects positively on your efforts and accomplishments, including:

- Letters of recognition from clients, other managers/executives in your company or industry, community personalities

- Clips of articles written about you or quoting you (even alumni news)
- Articles you have written and even copies of those submitted but not accepted
- Announcements or flyers or newsletters of any kind that throw a favorable light on your efforts, a speech you may have given or a public ceremony you participated in

FORTIFYING YOUR DEFENSIVE POSITION

Most people put more effort into plans for their vacations than they do their job defenses. They go with the flow, depending on traditional role models and expectations. It doesn't work that way anymore, as you saw in Chapter 2. You've got to plan your strategies for defending your job by focusing on four target areas—your superiors, your subordinates, your outside relationships, and your inner attitudes.

Since time immemorial, it's been accepted manager strategy: Make yourself more valuable by attacking your boss's problems. Find out what's bugging the bigwigs at your firm or in your division, and concoct a solution, or at least devise some suggestions. Now it may be easy if your boss comes to you and says, "Smithers, here's a problem; clear it up." But you can really pile up the appreciation points if you recognize on your own the larger problems your company's top executives face and take steps to help alleviate them.

Example: Goodrich & Sherwood, executive search and human resource consultants, discovered that the number one HRD problem worrying large corporations is identifying and efficiently managing personnel cutbacks and staff downsizing. It may seem ironic, but if you could prove your value in attacking this problem, you might prevent yourself from being swept out when the process actually occurs.

Or consider three other major headaches in the area of human resources that this survey uncovered:

1. Attracting, recruiting, and motivating skilled managers (again ironic, but have you got any motivation systems to suggest?)
2. Managing compensation and benefits under new tax laws to maintain executives and contain costs (if the tax law isn't your bailiwick, what about some cost-containment projects?)
3. Implementing cost-effective training to allow employees to move upward (can you offer new training techniques that don't cost big bucks—and that work?)

The point is, know what your boss's biggest problems are and try to solve them. You'll be appreciated.

Included as a target for your defensive activities are other managers and executives in different departments. Instead of working in competition with them, try to substitute coordination, with yourself as the leader. Stamp your department as a prime disseminator of information to other segments of the organization.

Break down the barriers with other departments by making them "customers" or "clients." Make everyone in your function a salesperson and a customer-service representative. Your department's reputation—and your own—will skyrocket.

"Operating down and laterally only is a big mistake that many managers make," opined one ex-executive who should know. You can't just have relations with colleagues, peers, and subordinates. You've got to hobnob in the business sense with those above you. Work on managing relationships with your direct and indirect superiors.

If that means doing favors, that's not all bad. It will help the company and it will certainly put you in a more favorable light. Playing politics is not a game. It's for real. View it positively. You find out what the actual system is at your firm, not the one outlined in the policy manual, and then work within it to produce pluses for your side.

To stay in command of your ship (or your function), don't neglect to go below decks. The buzz-phrase is "management by walking around" (MBWA). The reality is rolling up your sleeves and getting your hands dirty. Let your subordinates know you are willing to pitch in to help them, so they'll be more inclined to return the favor if you need them to defend your position.

Don't turn up your nose at "worker bee" assignments that involve lower management echelons. If the company is interested in better training programs, and you can help, raise your hand and offer to jump in.

There's a second buzz-term that is applicable here: "requisite variety." It refers to the concept that the more complex your actual problem, the greater the variety of sources you need for input to develop a successful solution. To bolster your prevent defense, the more and more varied backing you have, the better prepared you'll be. To elicit such advice, ask the entire staff under you to fill in a card with their answers to this question: "If I were in charge here, I'd . . ." Offer recognition and reward for the best suggestions, and make sure you respond to every one. This is not a substitute for suggestion systems—they work too. This is a personalized system of your own that helps build your stature in everyone's eyes.

Establish a two-way system of trust and loyalty with your troops. Don't adopt a "crack the whip" attitude to get better results. The Boston Celtics front office guru

Arnold "Red" Auerbach has this sage advice: "If you have employees who work through fear, you're not going to get any ingenuity out of them. You're not going to get employees who will take a gamble or come up with ideas. All you'll have are robots. . . ."

Take a new perspective on all your projects, from the interim report to the oral presentation to the monthly managers' meeting. Suppose top management were using just one project to be the deciding factor on whether to keep you or let you go. Would you do anything differently? Then do.

Got any dormant skills that have been lying around in your persona getting rusty? Usher 'em out and polish 'em up. Take advantage of temporary assignments to flash those skills around the organization. Stop hiding your light under a bushel. If you have a choice of several assignments, don't always take the back-room ones. Pluck a couple that will propel you to center stage.

Unspecialize. The more you can do these days, the better. Versatility is the key. Vary the areas in which you expand your talents. The sixth man in basketball, the utility infielder in baseball, the football player who goes both ways—all normally have longer careers than the pure shooter, the home run slugger, the fleet wide receiver.

Be an intrapreneur (another in the endless squadron of business buzzwords flying around these days, but appropriate here). As opposed to the business of being in business for yourself as an entrepreneur (see Chapter 11), the i-word refers to a style of operating that sets you apart. You accept the system of the organization in which you work, but you are propelled by the excitement of "your own business' (whether it's a two-person accounting department or a three-shift factory). It's an attitude toward work that marks you as a creative thinker, a risk taker, a challenge beater.

Develop an alternative career/sideline in your off

hours. Moonlighting at some aspect of your profession, or just tapping possibilities in your hobby or avocation, can make your mental and financial positions sturdier when your job prospects are shaky. If you're a financial manager, maybe you should explore tax preparation. If you're good with words, try offering your services as a business-news columnist or a local radio commentator/analyst.

Invest in yourself. Take some brush-up courses in your field. Go to seminars and professional association meetings on topical areas in your function and the industry as a whole.

Finally, work on your personality. Every little bit helps. A University of Michigan survey showed that over three-quarters of the respondents believe the reason people get ahead today is personality. Even if it's not completely true, the perception is there.

TARGETS OF OPPORTUNITY

To augment your defensive strategies, take the offense and look for areas of opportunity where you can improve your chances of retaining your job.

Don't be afraid to pursue lateral moves. Study the structure of your firm and hypothesize as to what layer or division you could realistically move to. Then keep an ear open for an opening. Even if you don't apply, note who does, and who eventually gets the post. If your firm offers dual-ladder career opportunities, investigate. A switch can rejuvenate your career.

Also keep a weather eye on reported trends and changing options. For example, Korn-Ferry, the big management consulting/executive search firm, and the UCLA Graduate School of Management identified the "fastest route to the top" in today's corporate world. It's through marketing/sales. Six years ago it was through finance/accounting. That doesn't mean you junk your accounting degree and head out into the field to sell. Just another bit of intelligence to file away.

With all this data tucked away in your mind's computer, you might decide you'd gain more ground faster in your dash for the top by moving elsewhere in the company. Three red lights: (1) Don't move to a position with less importance or authority, (2) don't move too far afield functionally without strong security, and (3) don't take a promotion or make a job change that leaves you in a position more vulnerable to the job ax.

One high-level manager interviewed for this book came in second in a two-man race for the next step to the top. His main drawback: "The other guy had slid from job to job. He had a lot more varied experiences, even involved in management consulting."

Said this expert on defensive survival: "If there's one piece of advice I'd give, it's to get different functional experiences . . . so you don't get pegged as a marketing professional, a computer expert, a human resource person. Mess around. Get experience in several fields. Also get involved in strategy development and organization planning, no matter how far down the chain of command. It'll all come in handy."

It may sound strange, but a "downsizing mode" at your own company can be turned to your advantage. Don't wait to be told to downsize your own operations. Take the initiative and investigate where cutbacks would be least painful. If necessary, prune pet projects, cut outside commitments of your own and your staff, try to accomplish more with fewer company resources. And make sure your plans—and the results—are broadcast to appropriate audiences!

You might even consider jumping ship with a lifesaver if you see downsizing becoming the operative trend at your firm. One manager saw cuts coming. He wasn't all that happy with his overall situation anyway. So he negotiated a split in which he continued to do his job—from home—for a lower salary and benefits. Both sides came out ahead. While his situation (internal editing) may have been unusual, keep it in the back of your mind when you're reading the handwriting on the wall.

PERSONAL SKILLS AS A DEFENSE

Personal skill building should be high on your list as an opportunity measure. Everything from the standard and the obvious (speaking, writing, listening) to the more nebulous (creativity, decision making) can be worked on.

Books and lecture halls aren't the only learning venues. You can become a better decision maker by studying in detail how another executive approached a problem, attacked it, solved it. The system is the key. Figure out how and why he made the decision he did, and try to transfer what you learn to your situation.

Same goes for creativity. Take a business problem, study it, then put it aside. Don't look for a solution in the immediate corporate world. Look elsewhere, in your everyday life, the magazines you read, the programs you watch and listen to. Utilize all your intellectual resources to come up with new ways to approach and resolve that business problem.

One of the most potent personal skills for the future manager will be language—a foreign one. As the global community shrinks and international ties expand, most viewers of the business scene agree that the ability to compete with foreign firms—sometimes on their own turf—is essential to long-term success. Yet few companies have a coterie of managers who speak foreign languages fluently, even ones who are currently stationed abroad.

The bottom line for you: Command of a foreign language can put you in command of a brighter future.

Consider polishing up that rusty *"se habla espanol"* from college days. You can take community college or university courses, buy some tapes on your own, or even hit a specialized language-tutoring school, like Berlitz.

Don't overlook *company programs* that can expand career options or enhance your skills. And don't just tap the standard stuff. Somewhere in your company there may be programs like these:

- Anheuser Busch employees were eligible to receive five days' training that qualified them to act as facilitators in company career-development workshops
- B.F. Goodrich offered a twelve-hour training program that taught managers to be more effective in career-related decisions with employees
- 3M gave a career growth workshop composed of twenty hours on company time and funded by individual departments

Even as you're making yourself more valuable to the company and less vulnerable to the downsizing broom, don't overlook the storm clouds that may be gathering.

RED FLAGS OF WARNING

"If you begin to suspect that your job is in jeopardy, you're probably right. If you think you've seen some signs, they're probably just the tip of the iceberg."

The person who said that didn't recognize the signs until it was too late. That's not to say he could have avoided the ax even if he had seen it poised over his job. But having your own early-warning systems will at least prepare you for what might be inevitable. And at most it could provide the impetus to either erect stronger defenses for yourself or bail out before being blown away.

The first thing to do is disabuse yourself of the notion that you or your function or department are just too valuable to be candidates for oblivion. Remember, even good performance is not an impregnable defense. So watch for those red flags a-flying. The second thing to remember is that they don't just march you up against a wall and rip the epaulets off your shoulders (or in this case snatch your key to the executive washroom). That comes later. First come the more subtle signs.

"Signals of doom" is what one terminated manager called them. He identified his as "downsizing of the company as a whole, divestiture within my particular division, moving a new guy in from another division with close responsibility lines to mine, watching as people began to take care of their own when staff reductions were in the offing."

Your signs may be different, and they may come from any of a variety of sources. The first place to look is close to home, at your personal relationships in the office. Ask yourself these questions:

- Does the boss spend less time with you than before, avoid you, turn to other people for solutions to his problems? Do you have personality conflicts with him, philosophical differences, strategy arguments?

- Are other managers making end runs around you to get to your subordinates in marked contrast to previous lines of command?

- Are you suffering more and more incursions by other managers on your formerly protected turf, without sufficient backup from your boss?

- Do your decisions/initiatives/suggestions suddenly start to hit stone walls or get slam-dunked back in your face with increasing regularity?

- Are you blocked from instituting changes in your

operations, from modifying systems to your standards and methods of managing?

- When you're trying to exert influence, do you feel
you're being treated like a lame-duck president?
- Do you feel your personal advancement in the
company has been put in a holding pattern?

Sometimes the signals of imminent change are more
general in nature, and can even be pretty easy to read.
For instance, when your boss is promoted—or fired—and
a new one is brought on board. Almost invariably there
is a housecleaning as the new coach brings in his own
assistants and even positive performers are put on waiv-
ers—simply because they're associated with the old re-
gime.

And sometimes you can overreact to what turn out
to be innocuous occurrences. Nevertheless, look out when:

- Headlines trumpet your industry's problems or its
appeal in takeover terms. If you picked up *Business Week* and saw your industry listed in the top
ten in merger and acquisition activity in the last
two years (as were banking, retailing, and others),
it should give you food for thought.
- You become persona non grata at meetings where
you used to be an integral part, or your projects
get put on hold and previous responsibilities get
shifted.
- Lots of other meetings are held behind closed doors,
and top management comes out asking for lists like
company credit-card holders and seniority dates.
- You start receiving inconsistent signals from superiors, colleagues, and even subordinates, a sense
of uneasiness creeps into your personal personnel
relationships, your person-to-person connections
become more strained and formal.

- You stop receiving consistent flows of needed information, and your complaints and requests are given short shrift.
- Someone in a seat of power with whom you formerly conversed in person and on the phone begins to send you memos.
- Your boss starts to pepper his compliments to you with the word but ("You did a fine job, but . . ."). Your butt may be on the line.
- Your boss turns up the heat, puts excessive and unnecessary pressure on you, gives you arbitrary and negative performance reviews.
- Or perhaps worst of all, the boss starts to ignore you.

When you start recognizing any of these signs in your work environment, remember the earlier quote—they could be just the tip of the iceberg.

CHARACTERISTICS TO CULTIVATE

Even after you've begun picking up danger signals on your personal sonar, all is not lost. A key part of managers' job defenses is to develop in themselves, and to display to top management, appropriate characteristics that are viewed as valuable to the organization.

The first thing is to determine which characteristics and managerial skills are expected of you by the company and which will enable you to contribute most effectively to the company's planned direction.

Each company is different, looking for different qualities, evaluating managers on different abilities. For example, IBM is reported to be looking for managers who can:

- Set performance plans
- Handle disciplinary matters
- Provide feedback on performance
- Explain key business decisions
- Emphasize quality

Similarly, RCA is looking at how well its managers:

- Select and utilize subordinate input about personal and career goals
- Look for ways to improve existing systems
- Take action on urgent requests
- Don't overdelegate to the point of losing control

If you haven't taken a reading on what your company is looking for in terms of its managerial makeup, there's no time like the present. And while you're deciding what it's looking for, give some thought to how you qualify. If you see a spot where you could strengthen your position, do it. The benefits will carry over to your new position in case those warning signals about the coming crunch were correct. Many companies, not just yours, are looking for qualities like the following in their managers.

Self-starters. Initiative has always ranked high as a positive quality for any employee level, but especially for managers. Find a series of projects that make sense for you—and the organization—especially those that sharpen other skills a company may value.

Flexibility. A prime requisite of any defense, especially when you're trying to retain your job. Be ready, willing, and able to take on new responsibilities, assignments, and even allegiances. Loyalty is nice, but when "the ship be sinking," it's every man for himself.

That doesn't mean you stab your boss in the back though, as reportedly happened to comedian and radio talk-show host Soupy Sales. A major New York City network gave him an ultimatum. Among other demands, he had to drop his two sidekicks. Sales refused. Principle. He was fired. Within a week, one of those sidekicks was offered Sales's position and took it. Money.

If your feet get held to the firing fire, you might also consider being flexible in terms of accepting a lower salary, relocation, and willingness to learn new skills.

4A's of achievers. Work on attitude, appearance, articulation, and accessibility. Take your cues from the leaders in your organization. If they project a rah-rah attitude, learn to cheerlead. If they roll up their sleeves and loosen their ties, get your hands on. If they can discuss the pros and cons of *The Organization Man,* start reading. If they can be reached by anyone with a problem, open your door.

Current. No one wants to be accused of obsolescence. And it's not just technical skills where managers fall behind. Sure it's nice to be up to speed on, say, computers. But it's just as important to be on top of new motivational techniques, the latest in negotiation tactics, the state-of-the-art in handling personnel problems and discipline procedures.

Johnnie (or Joanie) on the spot. When surveyed about their success, many executives admit they were in the right spot at the right time. But that's not all luck. It comes from being adaptable and having your fingers in a number of pies at the same time. It comes from being willing to assume different functional responsibilities, and taking on high-risk projects.

TAKING STOCK OF YOUR CURRENT POSITION

While you still have a job is the best time to take control of your career, analyzing where you are, where you want

to be, how you're going to get there, and most important, whether your current position is the best vehicle
for accomplishing that task.

You may decide that all these defensive measures
are unnecessary, that you don't need to look for warning
signals of potential job loss because this job isn't for you
anymore anyway.

In that case, you'd research your likes and dislikes,
goals and objectives, skills and abilities; decide where
you could best combine all these components; and make
the move. But that's another book.

Staying where you are also requires that you analyze your position thoroughly. You must find out how it
stacks up so you can implement your strategies for defending it. The first thing to do is conduct a six-month
checkup. Ask yourself the following tough questions at
least twice a year to see if your overall defenses are in
need of repair.

- Have I fallen behind my peer group in salary, title/
  position, scope of responsibility, recognition?
- Have I fallen behind in skill level, knowledge of
  technology, or management application?
- Have the company/division/functions changed so
  much I'm now out of step?
- Am I pulling my own weight, and is it recognized
  by top management that I am?
- What significant achievements have I chalked up
  recently, and where are my failures most apparent?
- Have I taken appropriate specific actions to capitalize on my strengths and shore up my weaknesses?

While that type of regular grilling will keep you on
track over the long term, a personal analysis inventory

for the immediately defensible future is necessary too. Suppose you were a corporate raider, and suppose you were checking the person holding your job, hypothetically speaking, of course. You'd be looking for bottom-line results, strategic fit, and, in true raider fashion, whether the job and the individual would be worth more to the company if either or both were lopped off.

Those are the ground rules. Now comes the acid test. If the questions in these three categories—career, personal, corporate—were asked of you, just how vulnerable would you judge your position to be?

Career

- Just how committed to this company is this person—and vice versa?
- What are this individual's career goals, how have they changed, and how do they fit in with the company's goals?
- Is this manager prepared to devote significant time and energy to both his or her own and the company's goals?
- Is this manager prepared to adjust personal objectives for company goals?
- Is the position this individual holds, and the one to which he or she aspires, the best fit for both person and organization?

Personal

- Where does this person stand in terms of age and salary scale relative to peers?
- Does he or she manage well up, down, and horizontally, with appropriate results reporting?
- Does this manager take advantage of every opportunity to become more valuable to the company

through training programs, attending conferences, making industry presentations, and the like?

- Does this person take advantage of opportunities to expand a personal repertoire of skills in areas such as speaking and writing?
- Does this individual's work-style fit the organization's—and vice versa?

Corporate

- What did this person's department contribute to the bottom line of the company?
- Would that function be labeled "support" or "optional" or "nice to have, but . . ."?
- How does this department stack up in overall terms in the company's rating system?
- What would a list of tangible results and achievements consist of?

NETWORKING AS YOUR SECOND JOB

"No matter where I work from now on, my second job will always be to keep networking with contacts in the industry. I don't want to get caught flatfooted if this ever happens again." So said one terminated manager who went on to find greener pastures.

Chapter 9 covers networking in detail in terms of what you do when you're looking for a new job. But it's the across-the-board opinion of ex-managers that networking must begin while an individual still has a job and continue indefinitely.

Basically your networking system under both circumstances (employed or unemployed) will be very similar. There are some differences, and certain aspects you should concentrate on while you're still "with job." For one thing, milk those telephones. No one is too unimportant to keep up with; no call is too unimportant to answer. Even people you don't know, or those trying to sell something, can represent opportunities for contact that can be tapped at later dates.

This is especially true of headhunters or recruiter calls. You may consider them a pain when safely ensconced in your job. But when you're out in the cold, these connections could stoke your job search. So be helpful and courteous to whomever you can. One rehired executive who has been through the entire experience says he now even tries to match other people with headhunters when he gets a call, because "you never know when you'll be in a similar position—again."

For another, be aggressive. While you're talking business with a client or industry colleague or a manager from another part of your company, probe for information you can file away in your "future prospects" file. You can be tactful and ask about industry trends and company directions without being blatant about wanting network knowledge to help protect your career.

For a third, exchange business cards with everyone, and keep your file of those one-by-two-inch cards current. They could be a gold mine for networking when you're out looking for work.

Finally, remember this advice that seems to capsulize today's management job situation. No matter what your defensive or offensive posture, keep your nose clean and your bags packed, because one never knows, does one?

CHAPTER 5

Let's Make a Deal

Turning the Discharge to Your Advantage

IF your defenses are breached, then at least make the best of a bad situation by getting the best benefits deal possible before you go.

Despite a growing trend toward uniformity, there is still no such thing as a typical benefits program for terminated managers. Some companies are generous, others frugal. Some industries are in a growth cycle, others in eclipse. Some reductions in force are widespread, others quite specific. Each termination situation is unique, and each company handles it in a little different manner. Just knowing that such is the case helps you put your own circumstances in a proper perspective. You'll also find it useful to know that there are some common denominators in the benefits field.

This chapter is designed to give you a brief overview of that field in relation to terminated managers. Sometimes there is no room for flexibility, no chance for negotiation. There are other times when a healthy dollop of benefits background will prove to be handy.

CLIMBING INTO THE BENEFITS RING

If your termination is not part of a larger program, like a prescribed RIF, you may be on your own as far as severance benefits are concerned. Then any negotiation with a former employer can turn into a real slugfest should either side be spoiling for a fight. While you may not want to be the aggressor, you should at least be aggressive. Here's the blow-by-blow of how one manager fought her benefits battle.

Round 1. The red flags of impending disaster had been flying for several months. A new president slapped everyone with nitpicking cost-cutting measures. The endangered manager saw and heard about line and staff individuals being discharged, apparently randomly, throughout the company. Then her secretary was dumped and no replacement was named.

When the ax finally fell on the manager herself, she went right to her boss and asked about the benefits due her. She had seen nothing in writing, and he was in the dark as well. So he bucked her on to Personnel, where she was put on hold for several days.

Round 2. As it turned out, the delay gave her a chance to marshall her forces. She asked around to find out what kind of deals other dismissed persons in the company were getting. She even went to axed managers she knew from other companies to inquire about their severance packages. And she read whatever she could lay her hands on regarding industry practices in general.

Round 3. Armed with a neatly typed checklist of negotiable items (which she refused to display to anyone), she sallied forth to do battle. Among the things she wanted were a month's severance pay for each year of service, extra time credited so her profit-sharing vested, a substantial bonus, earned vacation, dental as well as medical benefit extensions, letters of recommendation and outplacement.

Her jabs were met by heavy resistance. Six weeks' severance was the policy, no exceptions, she was told. No outplacement. Bonus payment depended on glowing report from former boss. A Mexican standoff.

Round 4. The fired and fiery female wheeled out the

heavy artillery. She pointed out to Personnel that she was not a run-of-the-mill employee but a decision-making, award-winning manager, one who had even earned her Ph.D. Then she hit Personnel with the haymaker. She was the only female manager of her rank in a company of 8,500 employees. And she was over forty years of age. The opponent began to see lawsuits dancing before his eyes.

Between rounds she rounded up helpful advice from a friendly attorney (who indicated that she didn't have all that strong a case for a better severance package). It didn't matter.

Final round. TKO to the dismissed manager. She got half a year in severance, the profit-sharing pie, a lump-sum bonus, two excellent letters of recommendation, and extended medical and dental paid for by the company.

PRENEGOTIATING HOMEWORK

Many managers are so dazed by the knockout punch of dismissal that they take what they are offered and walk. If your company's program is cast in concrete, or a specific reduction in force system is being implemented, then you may have no alternatives.

But if there's any flexibility, do some homework. Check employee handbooks, policy manuals, memorandum files, and other material the company hands out. See if you can uncover the answers to such benefit/severance questions as:

- Exactly what benefits are mandatory and how are they calculated? Is there any history of options or alternatives?
- How did your benefits accrue, from anniversary dates or on a calendar-year basis? Were any leaves

of absence or extended sick leaves involved? Are benefits calculated on salary, total earnings, a period average?

- Are there any restrictions or time limitations on the benefits in your package? For example, is there a cap on unused vacation time that you may have carried over from previous years?

- Are there negative ramifications if you're offered a different position in the same company and you decline? What happens in terms of benefits if you strike a consultant deal with your old firm?

- Are there any preconditions (such as joining a competitor) that will have an adverse effect on severance payments or extended benefits?

- Are there any policy phrases in any benefit or termination literature that you can use to advantage, such as "exceptions appropriate to individual situations"?

- If you are eligible for extended benefits, what is the time cap? Does that eligibility end when you accept another job? Are there "windows" that close if you don't take advantage of a voluntary separation program (VSP) or early-retirement offer?

Early retirement as a severance model

Those windows of opportunity that companies are throwing open these days to entice managers into early retirement may not strike your fancy. But don't ignore the packages themselves. There may be some details in them you can use to negotiate a better settlement of your own. Or they may give you some ammunition for providing alternative solutions in case of a negotiating impasse.

Kodak, for example, offered a package with a separation formula based on length of service with a maximum of fifty-two weeks' pay. There was also a pension-enhancement stipulation based on a combination of the employee's age and length of service.

Another example: A fifty-two-year-old with thirty-three years of service would have a total of eighty-five and be eligible for full-retirement income benefits with this particular program. Another example: A forty-seven-year-old with twenty-eight years would have seventy-five and be eligible for 50 percent. The plan also included four months of company-paid life, health, and dental.

Whether a program is labeled "early retirement" or "voluntary separation," you should give it a careful look. For one thing, it might foretell winds of change beginning to blow in your industry or company. For another, you should have as much "termination benefits data" stored in your personal knowledge bank as possible—just in case.

Actual program offerings

To gain the maximum knowledge, investigate not only what your own company is offering, but what other companies are putting on the benefit/severance table as well.

A typical voluntary separation program may include some or all of the following:

- Severance, such as one week's pay for every year of service up to twelve months (ask for enhanced severance by adding a specific number of years to actual service)
- "Retirement" benefits, such as continuation of life insurance or long-term disability (again, ask for extra credit)
- Lump-sum or bonus payments

- Career-transition counseling and placement assistance.

Some packages are labeled by number. One is referred to as 5-5-4. It's a generous VSP that adds five years to both age and service for pension calculations; four weeks per year to a maximum of twenty-four months as a cash separation payment; bridge payments prior to Social Security of 20 percent of base salary; continued health insurance; standard retirement benefits; one-on-one career counseling and extras (office, phone, computer) during the upcoming job search. It's hard to find any soft spots to negotiate in a package like that.

Remember, no separation package is exactly the same as any other. In fact, programs within the same firm may change from year to year depending on economic conditions and human resource requirements. Some companies implement a VSP and suffer by losing their more talented managers. They will have second thoughts about making their incentives too enticing.

Not only packages differ, but names and approaches can be very dissimilar. AT&T called its incentives for voluntary retirement its "Management Income Protection Plan." Polaroid at one point implemented a retirement-rehearsal program. Employees could "retire" for three months to see how well they adjusted before they made a decision on actual retirement. The point is that all packages and programs—including yours—have unique aspects:

- Sears offered half-pay for three years plus all accrued pension benefits in a lump sum.
- Xerox offered employees who were over fifty and had ten years of service an additional five years of age and service for calculating their benefits. Also any workers under sixty-two would receive a So-

cial Security supplement until they reached that cutoff point.

- General Electric offered one week's pay for each year of employment, accrued vacation, money in the profit-sharing plan tied to salary (including the company's contribution) plus interest, continued health and life insurance at no cost for a year, and, depending on length of service and age, the option of half-pay until retirement eligibility kicked in.

- Eastern Air Lines gave its managers salary for a two-week notice period, payment for unused vacation, and severance pay equal to one week for every year of employment at Eastern up to twenty-six weeks. Eastern also threw in the perk of "space available" passage on flights for those employees looking for jobs in other cities.

EXXON AT THE FOREFRONT

One of the most publicized and comprehensive termination programs to flash across the horizon was administered by Exxon. There were numerous parts to that program itself and many options in the packages offered. Various features of it were offered to more than 40,000 individuals at one time.

One voluntary-severance package was designed for managers too young to retire. A manager with twenty years' service got about one year's pay and benefits from an employees savings plan. Another focused on an older audience. A fifty-five-year-old making $50,000 with thirty years' service, for example, was offered an early-retirement plan that added three years of age and service to his record. That produced a pension of around $24,000 annually for life.

The list of specific booklets, seminars, and programs

offered by Exxon covers just about all the termination bases you could imagine, including:

- Exxon Career Continuation Counseling—outplacement offering with goal assessment, résumé preparation, interview training, and so forth
- Career Decision Workshops—to develop a personalized action plan by sorting through a full range of career options
- Retirement Planning Programs—concentrating on the financial aspects, with spouses invited
- Employee Health Advisory Program—counseling services extended six months after termination, dealing with family and marriage problems, alcohol, drugs, and life transition
- Managing Personal Transitions in Times of Change—to identify and better manage the personal issues and feelings that accompany organizational change, including stress inventory, transition planning, utilizing support services

All this and more for persons designated at that time to have "skills surplus to the organization" or "skills incompatible with changes."

CHECKLIST OF BENEFITS TO CHECK OUT

You can see from reviewing those programs that benefits in termination programs came in many different shapes and sizes. No matter what you are offered, you may be able to squeeze out more. But make sure you get at least the minimum of what's coming to you. Here's a brief checklist of common benefits:

- Separation payment or cash settlement

- Bonus (Christmas, quarterly, operating results)
- Pension payments and/or annuities
- Salary continuation or lump-sum payment
- Profit-sharing, thrift, and ESOP plans
- Credit for sick leave, personal days, vacation
- Time enhancements for pension vesting, severance payments
- Bridge payments related to Social Security
- Life insurance, maybe contributory group
- Long- and short-term disability
- Surgical, hospital, medical, dental, and health insurance extensions
- Discounts for car rentals, airplane fares, hotel reservations
- Options such as buying company car or computer
- Family counseling
- Personal, career-transition counseling
- Financial and employment counseling
- Recommendation letters, personal references/referrals
- Workshops for developing personal marketing plans
- Outplacement services or their equivalent (secretary, office, computer, copier, mail)
- Extension of notice.

KNOW YOUR RIGHTS—AND YOUR ACRONYMS

In recent years, the federal government has jumped feetfirst into the benefits fray and has had an impact on a number of the benefits on that list. The Tax Reform Act of 1986, for example, places new obstacles in the way of employers trying to sweeten the pot for early-retirement and voluntary-separation pensions. The government has whittled away at other economic incentives for early retirement with such actions as gradually raising the normal age for Social Security benefits from sixty-five to sixty-seven for those born after 1960. And Congress has even batted around the concept of portable pensions in its hallowed halls.

Perhaps the two best-known federal moves in the benefits arena in recent years are the Employee Retirement Income Security Act (ERISA) and the Consolidated Omnibus Budget Reconciliation Act (COBRA). Both statutes are too complicated to explain in a few paragraphs. Suffice it to say that if you think you're getting shortchanged in the benefits area, you may have legal recourse under ERISA. Many personnel managers think ERISA involves only pensions. That's not true according to interpretations by the courts.

Technically, ERISA covers employee welfare-benefit plans and employee pension-benefit plans. The first term covers employee benefits including medical, surgical, and hospital care, unemployment, vacation, and severance. The second term covers retirement income and deferred benefits.

ERISA doesn't tell the employer what benefits it must provide. So some employers think they can interpret policy and apply their benefit plans as they see fit. But practice has become an important component of policy in this issue.

It is noteworthy too that under ERISA, what the employer ordinarily *does* becomes just as binding as the published policy, plan, or program. In fact, those three P's needn't be published. They can be handwritten, unwritten, or verbally conveyed to managers. Even if a program or policy fails to satisfy ERISA's requirements, it still can fall under the ERISA cloak.

The most common problem occurs when a company decides to slice some executives from its payroll, realizes its severance plan would pay them big bucks, and so decides to change the plan. The company can't do that because of its fiduciary duty as administrator of the plan.

If you think you may have a case under ERISA, take these steps.

1. Check out the summary plan description and any other plan documents you received. They must be clear, plain, and complete. They should spell out all your rights and the company's obligations, including eligibility requirements, circumstances under which disqualification/forfeiture occur, and methods of qualifying for special benefits and exceptions.
2. Look into exceptions to the plans made for others. You have a right to know what the criteria are for gaining such treatment.
3. The old standby, see a good lawyer who has a solid background in this field.

Basically COBRA was designed to enable terminated employees to pay for continuance of certain benefits under their former employer's plan. Such employees can be charged up to 102 percent of the cost of such benefits as hospital, medical, surgical, dental, prescription drug, hearing, and vision group insurance plans. They can continue coverage for themselves and their insured dependents for eighteen months. Coverage may not be continued for those eligible for Medicare, if the person is covered by another plan, if the group plan terminates, or if the person stops paying the premium.

Ordinarily this cost will be a lot less than you'd pay for individual plans. In fact, some shrewd managers have turned this "right" into a negotiating chip when they're hustling for a job. This usually works best if you're looking to join a start-up venture. Such firms may not have health insurance plans. So you can offer to stay on your former employer's plan as long as COBRA requires and get your new employer to cover the cost, which should be much lower.

NEGOTIATING PLOYS IN TERMINATION

In most cases involving downsizing the number and type of benefits available to terminated managers are circumscribed by specific programs and detailed plans. Whether you have negotiating flexibility or not, you should include the following tips in your personal intelligence file for future reference.

- Always check out what other companies have offered in circumstances similar to yours. The more you know, the better your negotiating stance.
- Never sign anything without getting something in return. If your former employer wants you to sign a noncompete contract agreement, make it up the cash ante for leaving. Ditto if you're asked to sign a "no lawsuit" clause.
- Beware of ploys like this: A twenty-two-year veteran was offered nineteen weeks' severance. That was okay. But then the former employer withheld the equivalent of unemployment payments for that period, forcing the manager to stand in line to make up the difference.
- Take advantage of any "feelings" you're leaving behind—guilt, sympathy, empathy. If your former boss is suffering some pangs, ask for exceptions to standard offers. You may be the lucky one.
- Get copies of your Personnel file. In many states, the law obliges employers to let you see and copy it, even if your parting is not an amicable one. You

want to have in hand any commendations, awards, letters of praise, and such, to use in your job search.

- Ask for everything you're entitled to—and more. If your firm doesn't offer outplacement per se, ask for what outplacement usually provides, i.e., access to office space, telephone, computer, copier, and so forth. If you had a company car, ask if you can buy it or take over the lease at favorable rates. If the company bought you a computer to work on, see if you can buy it at a discount. Use your imagination.

- And use the imagination of other termination programs, like those you saw detailed earlier in this chapter. One company takes it upon itself to send out résumés of ex-employees, along with letters of praise reviewing individual strong points and suggesting where the employees might fit into the new organizations. No matter who handles recommendation letters, you or the company, try to get as many as you can from anyone who has a fancy title or some clout. They can open important doors. If you don't get such letters before you leave, you may find the reference door slammed shut as more and more companies, fearful of lawsuits for defamation, install policies of providing "directory information" (name, rank, and serial number) about departed employees.

  Another company sent out a "résumé book" to select firms. Does your company notify other employers about people or functions being cut? Some firms have gone so far as to take out tombstone ads (an unfortunate but appropriate monicker!) to let other companies know about talent they're cutting loose.

- Finally, don't go it alone. Talk with others leaving when you are. There is strength in numbers, especially if the adviser you hire is good with them.

UTILIZING SPECIALISTS

If you're able to extract financial counseling as a benefit from your former firm, you're one step ahead of the game right off the bat. If you can't, don't try to go it alone. Tax considerations alone are so confusing, you could end up with even worse problems than just being unemployed.

An accountant is a must. In fact, you should have a financial specialist look at your options and explain them to you before you start any negotiating with your former firm.

One of the major decisions you could face is how to accept severance, as a lump sum or in deferred payments. It's not as easy as determining "Do I need money right now or don't I?" You'll also have to consider the labyrinth of rules and regulations that emerged from the Tax Reform Act of 1986, especially concerning date changes in forward averaging rules, rollover possibilities, and the like.

Tax and financial specialists will be able to analyze your position, for example, on capital gains treatment. They'll know about the tax on early-retirement lump-sum amounts attributable to pre-1974 participation, and how that specialized relief gets phased out. They'll know the grandfather clause and age requirements that spare capital gains tax under certain conditions.

They'll be able to give you a specific game plan for investing and divesting. One fired manager took five straightforward steps after financial consultation. He:

1. Withdrew a certain percentage of his savings plan and left the rest to accumulate

2. Liquidated his spouse's entire pension plan

3. Refinanced his fixed mortgage to gain a measure of current monetary flexibility

4. Rolled over his IRA from matured certificates of deposit to more flexible IRA money market accounts

5. Headed straight for the state unemployment office

The last step may turn you off. "I have my pride," you contend. Put it in your pocket and see what you can buy with it. Look at it this way. You've contributed all your working life to that fund. Now it's your turn to get something back.

You'll be able to think up a hundred excuses for not signing up. You're too busy job hunting. It's dehumanizing to stand in line. You don't accept charity. The bottom line is that it's your money, you're entitled to it, and you can use it in your current position.

Each state has a different program and different requirements, so you'll have to check with the local office in your area. Is it worth it? A manager in Michigan lost his $75,000-per-year job, but found a check for $197 per week for twenty-six weeks. Not exactly tit for tat, but certainly better than ZERO!

If all else fails, and you get no satisfaction in benefits from your former firm, then you may have to consider courting a lawsuit.

CHAPTER 6

Don't Let Your Legal Rights Get Trampled On

Ducking the Golden Boot

WRONGFUL discharge lawsuits have become prime fodder for blaring seventy-two-point headlines all across the country. The media is awash with stories of million-dollar awards, bitter McCoy-Hatfield-like contract disputes, battles royal in the office and in the courtroom. So if you haven't been able to negotiate that sweet benefits package from Chapter 5, your next inclination may be to head for your local barrister's office.

In truth, most middle managers don't have a case when they are dismissed. For one thing, the hoopla surrounding dismissals generally causes companies to conduct those discharges strictly by the book. And for another, most middle management cuts are not caused by scheming executives wantonly flouting the law. They result from systematic reductions in force, a nasty draught of hemlock for both the employee and the employer, but one that can usually be defended in a court of law. Of course, there are exceptions.

This chapter doesn't advocate that you jump on the lawsuit bandwagon if you are, or become, a dismissed middle manager. It does recommend that you know your rights, that you recognize the difference between lawful and unlawful discharges, and that you be aware of the options—and the pitfalls—involved in contesting a dismissal.

CHANGING EMPLOYMENT ATTITUDES

Traditionally, executives have never been big on initiating legal action. That may be because they were usually the dumpers, not the dumpees. Or it may be that their parachutes were always a shade more golden than others'. Or it may be psychological, as one executive put it: "It'd be like suing your own father. . . , emotionally draining . . . and almost as damaging to your future outlook; you can be blacklisted very easily."

Whatever the case, traditions are changing. With the change has come a rapid deterioration in the traditional concept of employment-at-will, which states basically, "I hired you, I can fire you." Volley after volley of employee lawsuits bombardment has weakened that concept considerably. Basically the assault has come from five fronts.

Front #1—Public policy exceptions. This area developed to protect whistleblowers who exposed corporate wrongdoing, such as the individual who disclosed that his employer, a defense contractor, was falsely charging certain expenses to the government. Then there are those individuals who fulfilled public obligations, such as jury duty, and individuals who exercised certain government-governed rights, like collecting workmen's compensation, and were summarily fired for this action.

Front #2—Contract theory. More courts every day are finding binding agreements either expressed or implied in employer/employee relationships. Terms are usually found in employee handbooks, orientation sessions, and company policy manuals.

Front #3—Promissory estoppel. This legal doctrine holds that if an employer makes a promise, and the employee relies on it and suffers because of that, the former can be held liable for breaking that promise.

Front #4—Good faith and fair dealing. Each side in

a contract, even one implied in an employment agreement, is bound to conduct its activities under this stipulation.

Front #5—Abusive discharge. Another part of the
trend toward "fair," an employer can be subject to legal
action if it exhibits "extreme and outrageous" behavior
in its discharge process. This protects employees from
retaliatory firing and from suffering emotional distress
at the hands of employers.

As you can see, the field has blossomed. Not long
ago, age and broken written contracts were the basis of
the large majority of white-collar lawsuits. There are still
plenty of those around. Legal actions can run the gamut
from broken promises to privacy invasions. And sometimes even written documentation doesn't get in the way
of judicial judgments. Consider:

Promises, Promises

A national sales manager was offered a dream
job that turned into a nightmare. Visions of bonuses, stock options, and seven-figure salaries
danced in his head.

A business downturn, however, supplanted those
visions with the reality of less money, less power,
and eventually a lost job. The manager sued for
breach of contract and fraud. You promised, he
said. A jury agreed that he had been mistreated
and awarded him the equivalent of 120 years' annual salary (this award is being appealed).

Not Worth the Paper . . .

A New York State court heard another broken
promise claim. This case involved an oral, not a
written, contract. The litigant claimed he was offered job security, "unless he screwed up badly."
Normally New York won't hear an oral contract
argument unless it can be performed in less than

a year. We'll make an exception for oral employment agreements, said the court. On top of that, the employee had signed an agreement that he was hired under the employment-at-will concept and could be terminated at any time. No matter, said the court, as it awarded the discharged manager $300,000.

There are, of course, alternatives to such paralyzing cases. Besides simple negotiations, you should consider:

- *Alternate dispute resolution,* in which mediation and arbitration techniques are combined to save both sides time and money. You might find some creative solutions here that you wouldn't find in the courtroom. But if you're not ready to compromise, this approach won't work.

- *A summary jury trial,* where a six-person panel hears limited presentations from lawyers. The "jury" renders a nonbinding verdict which lays the basis and sets the parameters for a negotiated settlement.

- *Mini-trials* which mix arbitration techniques with aspects of the summary jury trial. There is limited access to opponent's facts, short presentations, and then a meeting of representatives of both sides to settle the dispute.

- *The private court system,* which has emerged as an alternative to the formal American judicial system. Used mostly to settle civil disputes, it's an idea that may grow as an alternative in a field dominated by the American Arbitration Association. One company, Judicate, went public in 1984 and after three years had offices in four major cities and a national system which was being used by insurance carriers, casinos, and others.

TO SUE OR NOT TO SUE

If you're convinced that nothing short of a full-blown, let-it-all-hang-out lawsuit will suffice in your case, there are several ways you can proceed. Naturally, the first step would be to hire a lawyer. Before you do that, you should brush up on a couple of areas. Start with the general employment characteristics that marked your last job. Then move on to age and performance appraisal before you head for the nearest lawyer.

Here are several general questions to get you thinking like a litigant:

- Did your former firm make a binding commitment to you in terms of length of employment or basis for discharge? (Look for the word "permanent" or the phrase "just cause" in the employee handbook.)
- Did it suggest that your employment was anything but at-will? Were any guarantees offered?
- Did it follow every policy to the letter in its discharge process? Was anything vague or misleading in any of those policies?
- Were any promises broken or agreements breached that might lead a court to judge the employer harshly? Can you prove what you assert?
- Was any bias (e.g., sex or race) exhibited in the choice of you for dismissal? Do you have suspicions, or facts?

But I Thought You Said . . .

A union worker saw his golden opportunity to climb the ladder to success when he was offered a job in management. He quit the union, became a manager, and was later fired. He sued, claiming that the company's general pattern of actions and policies indicated that he was reasonably sure of a job until retirement.

Not so, the company rebutted. You signed an employment-at-will agreement. Too bad, said the court. Oral and written promises which suggested lifetime employment overcome that written disclaimer.

MAKING A CASE FOR AGE

It's the law. You must not be discriminated against because of your age. And it's the first point most older ex-employees turn to when they decide to pursue their wrongful-discharge cases. In fact, age discrimination claims reportedly rose from about 11,000 in 1983 to 17,500 in '87. There are good reasons for that increase, including double damages in willful cases, right to jury trial, increasing average age of those juries, and increased willingness of companies to settle out of court.

Still it's not exactly cut and dried in the employee's favor. Because of publicity surrounding age cases, most companies have become much more sensitive to the issue and more careful in handling the discharge of older workers.

Most everyone today is aware of the Age Discrimination in Employment Act (ADEA) and the protection it affords the older worker. But you should also know about the areas where employers get an exception to the usual ADEA requirements. Basically there are four:

1. Bona Fide Occupation Qualification (BFOQ), where an employer can limit a job to workers of a certain age if it can prove age is truly a qualification (tough to do)

2. Reasonable Factors Other Than Age (RFOTA), in which a younger worker is chosen over an older worker for reasons other than age or cost, mostly

used in business cutbacks and reorganizations (more common)

3. Bona fide seniority system based on length of service

4. Bona fide employee benefit plan

The key concept to keep in mind in all instances is "bona fide." The employer can't use any exceptions as a subterfuge to get around ADEA requirements or a pretext to actually discriminate against an older worker.

Besides being aware of how the exceptions have an impact on your case, you've got to know about technicalities (filing with EEOC within 180 days, for example) and state variations (Oregon prohibits age discrimination against individuals from age eighteen on; Alabama has no age discrimination statutes). So you can see while age is the most visible area, it's not always that easy to crack. As in all legal endeavors, your best bet is a knowledgeable lawyer.

There are a number of things you can do to help determine if you have an age discrimination case and to fortify it if you do:

- Check on those exceptions. See if your former employer's RFOTA contained fair and nondiscriminatory standards and was actually and visibly applied. Make sure the bona fide in the other three exceptions were just that.

- Review the statistics. See if your company's RIF had a disparate impact on the older segment of the work force. Find out if it replaced you with a younger, lower-paid worker after it said your position was to be eliminated.

- Look for company policies (or the lack thereof) that reflect age insensitivity. Do any files contain statements that might indicate an age bias? Have there been comments that you can point to ("new blood" or "youth movement") that indicate discriminatory tendencies.

Stats and Words Combined

A fifty-six-year-old district sales manager heard the rumors. The youth movement was on, to keep the company in step with the times. Then came the employee's discharge, ostensibly because management wanted new people to reinvigorate the company.

When the ex-manager took the firm to court, though, it warbled a different tune. This time it contended that financial problems made it necessary to hire sales managers who could improve the company's performance.

Oh, yeah, said the court. Then how do you explain your actions in light of the fact that this discharged manager's sales results over the ten months before his dismissal were 10 percent higher than the company's average? The court's conclusion: age discrimination.

Look at your situation from the court's perspective. Besides legal language and requirements, there are overall considerations that can all add to or subtract from a strong case, such as:

- Was the employer fair in its discharge practices?
- Did it use reasonable and objective criteria in coming to employment decisions?
- Did it test the likely effects of the decisions before implementing them?
- Has the company been honest in its actions and dealings right down the line?
- Did it try to find new opportunities and other positions for terminated individuals, or did it toss them out on the street?

PERFORMANCE APPRAISAL IN DISCHARGE

The other general area that crops up in many legal briefs for discharged employees is performance appraisal—or lack of same. One jury decided that an executive had been "evaluated improperly" and tossed him a $61,000 bone.

That's the exception to the rule in most business reductions in force. Most often in cutbacks, performance appraisal isn't even mentioned as a factor in the discharge. It's strictly a question of economics. But if PA is brought up, you may have been handed a strong case for action. Ask yourself the following questions to lay the foundation.

1. Can management reconcile your performance appraisal record with the discharge? Did you have a series of satisfactory evaluations, commendations, and promotions before you were canned?

2. Do the criteria in the appraisals match policies in the employee handbook and personnel manual? Are the criteria objective and were they applied consistently in your case compared to others? Were the criteria subjective, or even possibly discriminatory?

3. Were you judged by any other standards not explained to you? Did your employer introduce those standards without your knowledge? Did appraisers suddenly and arbitrarily change their minds?

4. Did personal preferences or reactions enter into your appraisal? Were you given a chance to prove appraisals were biased or unfair?

5. Is the language in the evaluation system inconsistent with its numerical ratings? Do appraisers have the documentation to back up their decision?

6. Did management respect the privacy of your appraisal? Were details released to individuals without a business need-to-know?
7. Did the company use an obsolete job description as a basis for your appraisal?

Peeping Management

One of the most famous cases that involved performance appraisal in the discharge of a manager had all the makings of a Hollywood movie. The female manager had an impeccable record—consistently exceeding sales goals, receiving recognition awards and a $4,000 merit increase, even being accepted into the company's accelerated career-development program.

Her one crime—dating an individual who worked for the competition. Her options—stop dating or lose management status. Her decision—resign and sue. The court found in her favor, and her performance record weighed heavily in the decision.

CHOOSING THE RIGHT LAWYER

You may think you have a case based on those employment-at-will exceptions or age considerations or the performance-appraisal trends. But then, you don't have "Esq." after your name. You need an attorney, and despite the legions of lawyers in the United States, finding the right one for you can be like looking for the proverbial needle in the haystack. Before you start, keep a few truisms in mind.

It's your obligation to provide a candid and complete explanation of the facts of the case. Even the best lawyers in the land can't make chicken salad out of you-know-what.

You most likely need a specialist, someone who's had

experience in your type of case. That probably disqualifies Uncle John, your wife's nephew by marriage, and the legal beagle you play tennis with on Sundays (although they may be fine as sources for your search).

The better options for referrals, however, are business acquaintances and professional sources, such as other lawyers, court personnel, local judges, and the referral services of the local bar association. The best source, of course, is a manager who has already contested and won a wrongful-discharge case.

Finally, look before you leap. The first place to go is a library. You don't want to waste time and money, so do some homework on working with lawyers.

Books are plentiful. You could go straight to the American Bar Association for its *The American Lawyer: When and How to Use One.* Or you might prefer to thumb through Prentice-Hall's *Kill All the Lawyers? A Client's Guide to Hiring, Firing, Using and Suing Lawyers.* You also have the National Resource Center for Consumers of Legal Services in Washington to tap.

No matter how much or little lawyer research you do, your choice of legal representation will eventually come down to interviewing. And while experience and billing fees and resources are all important factors, the first thing you must do is feel personally comfortable with the person to whom you're entrusting your legal life.

As you carry on the preliminary discussion, keep track of your gut reactions. Does this individual's personality or manner turn you off? Do you sense interest in your case? Are your questions answered forthrightly or are you subject to double-(or triple-)talk? Do you feel you could be completely honest with this person?

Sometimes you can tell a book by its cover. Be aware of the office environment of your potential legal knight. It should be professional, orderly, and systematic, just like you want your case to be. Also, check for modern equipment, like word processors. In this day and age, typewritten preparation of legal documents is like sailing that slow boat to China.

Ask about clients and past cases. What services are generally provided in such cases? Who would work on such a case? Who and what would be involved in courtroom representation and hearing attendance? Also, what will the system of communications be like? How often will you meet? What sort of updates will you receive? Will you get copies of all documents prepared for your case?

GETTING DOWN TO THE NITTY-GRITTY

Once you decide to hire, the meter starts to run. So you'd best have all your questions out of the way before you discuss the nuts and bolts of the case.

Before anything happens, present a brief outline of your circumstances, and get a handle on the monetary aspects of proceeding. There's no sense forging ahead if such an action is going to land you in the poorhouse. And you don't want any unforeseen expenses muddying up your future relationships with legal counsel. Make sure you hit these topics:

- After discussing strengths and weaknesses of the case, ask for a list of scenarios and likely outcomes, and estimates of time and workload for each such settlement.
- Check billing rates, whether they are negotiable and if a flat-fee option exists; also billing procedures, how much you have to pay and when. You may want to ask for a letter of engagement laying out these items.
- Ask about monetary differentials among senior and junior partners, associates, and paralegals. If you're paying by the hour, you don't want to be charged

full-time lawyer rates when the work (research, interviews) is being done by a paralegal or clerk.

- Probe for any hidden costs, like document-copying or mailing/messenger costs. Do rates include overhead and incidentals? What about the cost of expert witnesses or transcripts?

- Keep a wary eye on procedures. Are there any limits on items that could have an impact on your expenses, such as traveling first class, computerized research, or overtime? Do they assign two lawyers to take depositions and interview when one would seem sufficient? Do they itemize all their bills so you know exactly what you're paying for, and so there is no duplication?

"Aha," you say, "Now that I know about all these good bases for lawsuits, and the way to pick a winning lawyer, I'm sure I can be a big winner in employment litigation warfare." Before you pull the trigger, better consider some of the darker aspects of such legal actions.

Time. First you have the amount of time you personally have to spend collecting material and building a case. Then there's the lawyer's time, which of course you pay for. Also, there's the court time. It was estimated that one in five Americans would jam the judicial system with a civil lawsuit in 1987. Can you afford to wait in line?

Cost. Naturally the lawyer will want his cut of the action, and you may have to put up some up-front money too. But what about other expenses—copying documents, travel for interviews, accountant, other out-of-pocket. Are you willing to commit whatever financial resources are necessary to win?

Opposition. You may be going up against a hardened court opponent with high-powered legal help and almost unlimited resources. Pugnacious resistance may be their middle names. On the other hand, your foe may not have the proverbial pot to pee in. In that case, even a victory in court may turn out Pyrrhic in nature. Just how deep are those pockets you're reaching into?

Unpredictability. Even a savant like Jeanne Dixon can't predict how today's courts will react tomorrow. The field of employee litigation is littered with the bodies of ex-employees who were certain their cases were foolproof. There are significant variations from state to state in both actual laws and judicial trends. Michigan and California are generally considered the most liberal and unpredictable, while Alabama is seen as a bastion of the employer.

Psychological. As the quote in the front of this chapter put it, you'll be going after an important piece of yourself in the person of your former employer. Remember the look on Luke Skywalker's face when he initially cut off the head of Darth Vadar only to see his own visage staring up at him from the detached helmet? Are you psychologically prepared to sue "your father."

Privacy. Suppose your opponent comes back at you with all guns blazing. That means every aspect of your former business existence will be dragged into the open. If you have even the tiniest skeleton bone hiding in your career closet, it could be paraded out for all the world and your next potential employer to see. Can you think of any facts you'd rather not see go public?

Probing the Employer's Soft Underbelly

If you've decided that you've been subject to wrongful discharge, and those darker features of litigation don't put you off, then you can start looking for vulnerable spots in your former employer's position. You already know the five main exceptions to employment-at-will and the general considerations of age and performance appraisal that may apply to situations similar to yours.

The following is a brief review of where employer practices most often suffer incursions from discharged employees' attacks. Keep them in mind when you're mounting your own.

1. *Employee handbook.* The number-one culprit in many cases, with "just cause" being the phrase most often picked on. Ex-employees are claiming the handbook serves as a contract, and the employer must abide by its policies on discipline, performance appraisal, and especially terminations. Look for suggestions of guaranteed employment, deviations from policy, discrepancies between handbook and job-application blanks.

2. *Privacy.* A growing scourge for the employer, especially in the reference area where slander, defamation, and libel crop up. You may have the makings of a case if you (a) were fired for an off-the-job dalliance (the company can't impose its notions of morality on you), (b) were fired with unnecessary fanfare in front of colleagues, (c) were the subject of public disclosure of private facts upon discharge, (d) were placed in a false light by management's utterances, or (e) were badmouthed by management to a portion of the employee work force.

3. *Timing.* Most employers are very careful in this area today. ERISA regulations make them so, especially since those federal statutes supercede the states'. You may have the basis for a suit if you were discharged relatively close to (a) becoming vested in a pension plan, (b) becoming eligible for a big bonus (or a small one, for that matter), (c) becoming eligible for enhanced pension benefits.

Bleep the Bonus

A regional salesperson rubbed his hands in glee at the news. His company had sold a cool $5 million worth of equipment in his territory. According to his contract, he was due a hunk of change as bonus, somewhere in the neighborhood of $100,000. A nice neighborhood, indeed.

When the boss called him into headquarters, the salesman figured it was to talk bonus. Instead, it was to talk walking papers. After twenty-five years of service, the salesman wondered, "Why now?" He suspected it was to avoid paying him the bonus. The court shared his suspicions and ruled the company had broken "an implied covenant of good faith and fair dealing."

4. *Personnel records.* Another area for close scrutiny, especially concerning what information the company has collected in your file, how it was used, and to whom it was disclosed. If your employer based its firing decision on inaccurate, outdated, or inappropriate material, there could be trouble in River City. Check for harsh language that might indicate personal bias, good performance reviews that preceded a "You're an underperformer" firing, and whether the employer didn't follow company policies or state laws in its collection/disclosure procedures. If it failed to use due care in protecting your file or limited your access to it (check state laws), the firm may also be liable for action.

Amicably—Into Court

When business went sour, a paper manufacturer had to cut its sales force. "I understand," said one employee who was let go. "I'll go quietly." "Here," said the company, "take this glowing letter of recommendation and this letter of introduction too."

A few months of fruitless searching later, the ex-employee found out that the company had sent a report to the local credit bureau indicating that the mutually agreed-on separation was caused by a poor sales record on the employee's part. In the lawsuit that followed, the court judged the company guilty of careless handling of the employee's records.

5. *Policies.* Make sure your former employer followed all of them to the letter, particularly termination. Courts will ask if the policies are fair, if they were applied consistently, if there is sufficient written documentation and verbal reinforcement. You be the judge and probe those questions in your situation.

6. *Lies and promises.* Usually based in written company documents like a handbook, but can be oral in nature. Check for publicly announced stances ("We encourage long-term employment"), established practices ("We only fire for just cause"), and oral assurances that you have relied on ("You'll have a permanent position if you move to Oshkosh"). Also, you might consider asking for the reasons you were fired, in writing. If management lies or uses pretexts, you'll have more ammunition for your cause. Sometimes you can be defamed by a false impression left by something an ex-employer says, even though it's technically true. For example:

You Can Look It Up

A Wisconsin employer told a reporter that an employee had been "terminated." Strictly speaking, as he pointed out in court after being sued for defamation, he was correct. Termination can apply to either kind of separation, voluntary or involuntary.

That may be technically true, said a court. But that specific word left the impression that the employee was fired, which was not true. Post a W in the victory column for the employee.

CUTTING THE CORD—LEGALLY

One last legal option you should know something about is the discharge release. It's a protective device used by companies to avoid the types of lawsuits a white-collar worker is likely to initiate. It may not be a bad step for you to take, either, especially if you're not sure how strong a case you have, or if any of those negative aspects of litigation mentioned earlier hit close to home.

Before you even consider signing a release, make sure:

- You are being offered more than the normal severance package—it's got to be sweet
- You ask your ex-employer every question that comes to mind, from tax withholding to deferred payments
- You see if you can get nonmonetary concessions, such as a promise not to give out unfavorable references
- You get enough time to consider all your options
- You find out what the company has offered others in similar situations as inducements, and how those individuals handled those offers

Besides common sense, there are other strong reasons for that last step. It's a tricky field and an expert will know where the mines are planted. For example, certain states have their own quirks where releases are concerned. California has a labor statute that says if the employer holds up pay while requesting a release, not only can the release be declared invalid, but the employer could face criminal charges.

Federal agencies also poke their noses into release situations. You may be asked to give up a right established by law (suing for age, race, sex discrimination). In that case, the agency with jurisdiction often has its own requirements which must be met before a release is acceptable. For example, if you're asked to withdraw an age discrimination suit pending before the EEOC prior to signing a release, the EEOC must agree to that withdrawal step before any dotted lines can be signed on.

All in all, conducting a major lawsuit is a tough way to make a buck. In the massive middle-manager layoffs which have been going on, few individuals have prevailed in court. It may be best to just put the whole nasty experience behind you, and start sifting through your options and opportunities available for getting on with your career.

CHAPTER 7

The Outlook for Today's Manager

There Is A Light at the End of the Tunnel

BEFORE you stroll through the specific options and opportunities for managers outlined in Chapter 8, take a look at the silver lining that has begun to appear amidst all the clouds of gloom and doom in downsizing and termination.

You've read in earlier chapters about the causes and effects of the squeeze on middle managers. This chapter turns to the present to probe into the sometimes too dimly lit corners of the employment outlook for middle managers.

"Brains and wit will beat capital spending ten times out of ten," says Ross Perot, the iconoclastic former head of Electronic Data Systems. He founded that data processing company and then sold it to General Motors Corporation.

Perot could have been speaking about his own finely honed intellect and keen senses. He could also have been speaking about his talented teammates as they built EDS from an idea to an exceptionally successful company.

But he was not heaping praise on his associates or himself. In fact, he was, while still serving his tumultuous tenure on GM's Board of Directors, jabbing a barbed harpoon at the corporation. He aimed to pinpoint the key lesson that it should learn from its joint venture with Japan's largest auto manufacturer, Toyota.

Perot was speaking about GM's present results from automating its plants. The two companies joined to form the New United Motor Manufacturing Inc., Nummi for short. The venture, whose name has a more oriental than western sound to it, was to turn out the Corolla-based Chevy Nova. GM contributed to the investment a shuttered, aging plant located in Fremont, California. Toyota provided a cadre of Japanese top managers fully indoctrinated in their native country's managing styles. The plant, significantly, was unstuffed with robots or other new-wave, high-tech gadgetry when it opened.

This nucleus, along with a converted covey of American managers, supervisors, and workers, used brains and wit to create a new auto manufacturing unit within the old shell. Its productivity immediately scored double that of most of GM's other plants. Moreover, the newfound quality of Novas cruising out of Fremont earned customer satisfaction ratings higher than any GM car. And, to warm the frigid hearts of the corporate cost-cutters at headquarters, these natty Novas rang up the lowest warranty repair expenses among GM's entire fleet.

The word from out Fremont way spread too slowly to save GM from drastic personnel cutbacks among middle managers and workers. After all, it's about as easy to get a gigantic corporation to shake off sixty years' accumulation of managerial rust as it is to teach an elephant to tap-dance.

The lessons of Nummi
AND THE NEW WORKPLACE

What is vital for senior managers everywhere to get a handle on is that technological developments require managing, just as people do. It's all well and good for cost-conscious executives to be pleased that the robots will keep working efficiently even after they flick the switch to turn off the lights on the factory floor. And it is comforting for them to know that idling robots to reduce output causes far less pain to everyone—executives, managers and workers alike—than paring more people from the payroll.

Yet it is a fact that GM, whose size exposes it as a glaring example, invested $40 billion (enough to buy outright two or three Japanese auto companies) to robotize and computerize plants to increase their productivity. It is also a fact that thus far this huge investment has been about as useful to GM as it would have been for the captain of the *Titanic* to order the stewards to shift the deck chairs in order to trim ship. One of the lessons of Nummi is that it's not simply automating that gets results. It's the act of managing new technology that really counts.

That's not to slam-dunk GM alone. Many other companies have in similar fashion egregiously misemployed capital. What's exciting for the job outlook for you and other middle managers is that the experiences with automation and computerization are now flashing green lights of opportunity. They're no longer signaling new dangers of displacement as discussed in Chapter 2. These "go" signs beckon you to seize control of the asylum before the programmed automatons wreck the manufacturing and office systems they're capable of improving.

The crucial lesson from Nummi: the most productive workplaces are people-oriented. That's not to say that Fremont has no modern equipment. But the plant is not overburdened with technology. The plant's success is teaching managers how to marry technical equipment to personnel.

A decade ago, when the ubiquitous computer first began to appear in nearly every office and its terminals began popping up on factory floors, many managements jumped on the bandwagon with a vengeance, deciding that automation was the answer to failing competitiveness, declining productivity, and soaring wage and salary costs. In fits of problem solving and decision making, they opted to throw huge sums of capital into the pot to buy the right kinds of equipment to speed up the solution.

They neglected to hire managers to stir up the capital in that pot, however. The results they achieved were akin to that kind vintners get by dumping excess yeast into wine vats to hasten fermentation. These executives achieved equally predictable vinegary effects on the quality of manufacturing and office output.

Most executives gave too little attention to the fact that your changing workplace requires changed management methods and styles. If they automate the factory or office, for example, to get it to work well, that requires pairing the equipment with people, not paring the human element. The pairing with an "i" requires managers to plan, organize, support, and coordinate—which is exactly what you and other managers have been doing since the time when the head cavemen sent out scouts to locate the meat on the hoof, then directed the spear throwers to the slaying site, and coordinated the transportation of "material" back to "headquarters."

The need to utilize proven managerial skills in a technologically oriented age provides great opportunities for you and other current managers. Some of you may need to shape your styles and methods more than to change your functions. But, it's a grave mistake to eliminate managers altogether. To get new high-tech equipment on line, companies must use your human skills along with technology. You, as a middle manager, already have the necessary skills and experiences to plan and organize that requisite pairing of people with new, automated machinery.

HELP WANTED: MANAGING SKILLS

Much static about organizational structure has crackled through the ether during this crash period of corporate downsizing. Some students of business structures call it flattening the managerial pyramid or delayering management. Some companies have even eliminated whole internal functions and contracted out their tasks.

GE, for instance, swept away its entire News Bureau. It functioned in much the same way as do independent public relations firms. Rather than giving its product and location managers a choice between using the News Bureau or an outside PR firm, GE axed the option. The PR work and the jobs that go with it, though, have simply shifted from within the company to outside. That action hurt GE managers and employees in the News Bureau. It created new jobs at PR firms.

Some analytical observers cite such layoffs as a way to cut excess organizational fat. However, it's likely that the payroll cost savings of GE's action will pop up in accounts payable in the guise of billings from PR consultants. The net savings may be nil. Yet for appearances' sake, management can now say that it's leaner and meaner.

The good news here, though, that offers opportunities for displaced managers and hope for those still employed, is that old business structures are changing. Better-trained and educated workers use more brainpower than brawn to operate automated equipment. They now interpret and react to computer-generated information received directly from terminals and thus bypass the old managerial hierarchy.

These "knowledge workers," as they are titled by some management gurus, now make many operating decisions. Their managers in the new structure take roles supporting the workers as planners rather than acting as old-time "Do it my way or you're fired" bosses. Such new-style managers are, especially in this time of revolutionary change, needed more than ever. History shows that structural changes always open up new opportunities and create new jobs.

You, like many middle-level managers, may have been brought up with a picture of the organization as a specific structure. The plant superintendent had, in such organizations, X number of general foremen as subordinates. Each general foreman had X number of supervisors to manage who, in turn, had X number of workers beneath them. That neat pile of organizational boxes doesn't work so well when knowledge workers take over the workplace. Staff specialists in old organizations—such as industrial engineers, trainers, and personnel people—devised work flows, trained employees, and advised. They did not operate.

The modern organization structure, though, needs support from managers with *operating,* hands-on experience, not purely stafflike advisory capacities. In the operating areas many displaced managers have the greatest experience and skills. Modern-day workplaces need those skills to be sure that the right decisions on work flows and job design are made. They can't be made by people who visit the workplace so seldom that they need a guided tour to avoid getting lost.

THE JOB-SATISFACTION QUOTIENT

Another vital requirement of the new workplaces is for managers to improve job satisfaction, both among their workers and in their own jobs. One think tank estimates that colleges and universities are turning out 30 to 50 percent more graduates than there are suitable jobs. Many "overqualified" graduates, they say, will never ascend the traditional managerial ladder—simply too few rungs available, and those that exist are already overcrowded. Many of those who may have aspired to become bosses will remain skilled employees. Even some current managers may find that they have no further room to grow. Some individuals may stay in the same jobs for ten, even twenty, years to come.

To motivate individuals caught in this vise requires that satisfactions be built into the job itself. They'll no longer get their kicks from quick-step promotions. Here, again, you'll find that great opportunities and challenges await managers with long-term operating experience.

When time and tides sweep away the muddy puddles created by hasty personnel upheavals, senior managements will find that their axes and adzes have shaved the middle levels too lean. Many companies are already squeezed by the shortage of experienced operating managers.

Such companies can't reach out to recall the departed managers. Drake Beam Morin, Inc., claims that 85 percent of its clients find new jobs at salaries equal to or better than the ones they lost. Those individuals are not about to return to the companies that kicked them out. (More on how managers like you accomplished this feat appears in later chapters.)

REDEPLOYMENT OF MANAGERS SPEEDS UP

Generalizing about improved opportunities for middle managers may not provide all that much solace if you're among the ranks of the discharged. That's especially true if you've been cranking out résumés in quantity (one manager reportedly kept a meticulous count—it came to 3,376) and pounding the pavements from one job-seeking stab to another.

So, how about this specific. In an interview for this book about the job outlook for discharged managers, James E. Challenger, president of Chicago-based outplacement firm Challenger, Gray and Christmas Inc. asserted firmly: "The time gap for finding new jobs is lessening. We've been tracking for ten years how long it takes for our clients to get placed. One big change lately is that the difference in months has grown shorter between the time it takes for managers over fifty to find new jobs compared to those under fifty. At one time we calculated that it took older managers one month longer to get new jobs compared to the younger ones. That's a third longer—from, say, an average of 3.2 months to 4.2 months. But that gap no longer exists. At worst it's a week."

Challenger maintains that change indicates a trend among companies toward hiring more mature managers rather than snapping up the baby-boomers or job-hopping fast-track kids. "But before giving you some reasons for that trend, here's two more facts about the jobs we help individuals to get with our outplacement services. The first is that more of them are moving to companies smaller than the outfits that fired them. The second is that our clients are relocating geographically more frequently than before. I can only really speak about the major employment areas, not small cities or towns. About 35 to 40 percent are moving to new geographical locations. It used to be one in five.

"Corporations think that they're getting more stability when they hire older managers. If they hire individuals in their twenties or thirties, they'll have them for maybe five years. When they hire people in their forties or fifties, they believe they've got them for fifteen or more years. These older managers bring more experience to the job. That lessens the margin for error in picking the right persons for the right positions. Also, they're more flexible and they adapt better to change."

Any way to document those beliefs that mature managers can adapt more easily?

"I don't have any statistics that would be reliable measures of that," said Challenger. "My sample would be too small. Our company works with 1,500 individuals a year to get them into new jobs. We only get two or three a year who bounce back from their new employment—actually we don't really track them. So I really don't know. But I think these small numbers indicate that they must satisfactorily adapt to the new workplaces and their new managements."

Other factors are at work beyond those cited by Challenger. When economic conditions are difficult, for instance, companies give more weight to your experience when they hire. Those individuals who have managed, as is most likely your case, through wars, skyrocketing inflation and interest rates, energy shortages, and other crises have had baptisms of fire. That's of incalculable value when you're compared to people who only achieved managerial status during the 1980s.

In addition, people like Ronald Reagan and Chrysler's Lee Iacocca have created new respect for older role models. Some senior executives have spoken openly about their disenchantment with the new "kiddie corps" of potential executives and feel that youth has been wasted on many of them.

One such executive was heard saying, "Those damn Harvard and Stanford MBAs are overpaid, overtrained, and over here. They come in expecting to be made president of the company a couple of years after we hire them. I'm going to look for some 'steady Eddies' that I can rely on. Let those fast-track kids crunch numbers down on Wall Street with the rest of that bunch. They deserve each other."

The upside of downsize

Chapter 2 gave you a bushelful of social and economic reasons behind downsizing and managers' layoffs. They are all beyond the direct control of middle managers.

Many senior executives of very large companies, those who have the power to control the destiny of the corporations they run, gave in to the herd instinct. When they saw major concerns hack and slash away at payroll, they acted first (downsized) and looked later (effects on operations). That's the reverse of the old axiom "look before you leap."

There are now many encouraging signs that such executives are at least attempting to put Humpty Dumpty back together again. That augers well for the future employment opportunities for you and other middle managers. It's good news for the economy and for most companies, too. Actions of top managers are mirroring a basic law of physics—every action ultimately produces an equal and opposite reaction. For example, many of the same companies which rushed to deplete their managerial ranks through separation-incentive programs, elimination of functions, and freezes on hiring are now becoming involved in "revitalization."

One thrust of this concept is to restore the morale and productivity of the remaining mid-managers. Even with all the cutting that's occurred, far more managers have stayed in their jobs than have been displaced. Whatever actions are taken that have positive effects on this group of survivors will be important factors in how well their companies operate.

At least part of the process of revitalization takes place naturally. It results from changed "job descriptions" of the survivors. As fewer middle managers cover wider areas of the business, they automatically broaden their scopes of responsibility. Fewer levels of management allow individuals in the middle to reach farther down into the organization. At the same time they relate more closely to the senior, policy-making executives at the top.

Belated though the recognition is, companies are now more aware that middle managers require wider knowledge of the functions of business. They need more than ever before to improve their human-relations skills, get more understanding of technology, and of financial management. Ironically, the new knowledge and skills that companies need are easily available. You, like many middle managers, may already possess them.

In the past, unfortunately, corporations have substantially underutilized their middle managers' talents. The "new look" created by restructurings results in fuller use of the capabilities of the individuals in the middle levels of management. That, too, brightens the outlook for redeployment of skilled managers.

Consultants are being retained to look at the needs of client corporations for job redesign and to suggest new management structures. They're assessing the abilities of managers—to be sure that the companies have them in suitable slots from which they can make the greatest contributions.

Even more gratifying for middle managers is the fact that job enlargement usually means job enrichment. When you're no longer confined to one narrow duty or function, you experience increased job satisfaction. This is vitally important. It's true that most managers reach a plateau. That's inevitable because the managerial ladder narrows as it approaches the top.

Increased job satisfaction keeps middle managers in their forties and fifties committed and challenged throughout their careers. Those feelings offset the downer that comes one day when they realize that they have been passed over for any real chance to reach the executive suite. When such managers are motivated, though, they become more valuable. Corporations increasingly rely on them to develop the next generation of managers. Increased reliance boosts the security of the surviving managers, as well as their feelings of self-worth.

Soon you can once again dream the old American Dream of long-term, satisfying careers uninterrupted by the traumas of displacement. You'll feel growing hope in the corporate workplace for a restoration of corporate loyalty to managers and employee loyalty to companies, both of which crumbled under downsizing. Psychologists say that middle managers still yearn for a bonding with their companies. The outlook is that the developing "re-reliance" of the two parties upon each other is becoming a "re-reality".

HEY, WAIT A MINUTE!

There's no shortage of doors at which to lay the blame for the dislocations caused by the restructurings of American industry. The leaders of the largest companies have been just as quick to shuck off responsibility for downsizing as they have been to wield the ax on middle-management employment. Where do they place the blame? Squarely on the shoulders of invading hordes of competitors from abroad. They've openly pleaded from every available pulpit for U.S. government protection against foreign competition, foreign investment, and hostile takeovers.

Some business executives have even formed an uneasy alliance with their traditional adversaries, the labor leaders. They've joined to rail against imports, which, they say, are causing the McDonaldization of America. The U.S. is in danger of becoming, if their doomsday predictions are to be believed, a nation of hamburger flippers.

But wait a minute. This nation has not abandoned manufacturing to foreign firms. Bureau of Labor Statistics studies show that manufacturing output remains at approximately 21 percent of gross national product, a percentage which hasn't appreciably jiggled on the charts since the end of World War II. GNP has grown since then. So have manufacturing jobs, albeit at a slower rate than those in the service sectors.

What has taken place, of course, is a huge shift in employment from the old rust-belt manufacturers like steel to new industries—pharmaceuticals, computers and high-tech components. Even in steel, output and employment have hopped, skipped, and jumped from the huge, vertically integrated Bethlehem and USX-type companies to smaller, specialized mini-mills.

Those new mills are much more efficient. They can more easily and quickly respond to market demands than the aging hulks whose business they've stolen. Moreover, the mini-mills have recaptured from foreign competitors some of the market share scrapped by the giants. There's a very large message in the growth of steel-making mini-mills for executives who whine that they can't compete with foreign industry.

About complaints that foreign investors are taking over American business, one executive says, "I don't give a damn who owns the business as long as it's successful." The plain fact is that for the first 100-plus years of its existence, American businesses were owned primarily by foreign interests. During that time the U.S. was transformed from an agrarian economy to the most powerful industrial nation on earth. Was that foreign ownership a drag on the country then?

Looking at the flip side, companies like Coca-Cola, Singer, Ford and other multinationals have benefited the rest of the world by investing in other countries. So large was the investment flow from this country into foreign operations in the 1960s that the Johnson administration put restrictions on it for fear the outflow of capital would result in job losses in the U.S.

Today, some stump speakers object, the inflow of investment from abroad may have a negative impact on jobs. They fear that the investors who own U.S.-based operations may suddenly pull out. Nonsense. It's hard to remove bricks and mortar already in place. Let the doomsayers also remember that while foreign investors like Mitsubishi (Japan) in Minnesota, Hoescht (W. Germany) in New York, or BOC International (Great Britain) in California repatriate their profits, that's a small bag of money compared to the wages they pay, the values they add, and the jobs they create. They can sell their investments, but the buildings, equipment, and jobs stay here.

It is also estimated that foreign investors supply almost one-quarter of the venture capital in the U.S. That's capital used to start up new businesses which create new opportunities and jobs, especially for the dispossessed but experienced middle managers like yourself. The money from abroad considerably enhances the economy of our country. It brightens the outlook, options, and opportunities for employment of managers and workers at every level.

But what about the seldom challenged statements that America is becoming a service-dominated economy and that service companies provide nothing but minimum-wage jobs? The rebuttal is that manufacturing itself has grown to fill the needs of the service sectors.

IBM, for instance, an acknowledged leading manufacturing company, needs increasing services for its customers—applications engineering and software programming (highly paid jobs, incidentally) to name two. Moreover, IBM is itself a service-oriented company and is a part of the service as well as the manufacturing sector.

The fast-food chains, butt of the most derisive wisecracks about service companies for their low-wage profiles, buy grills, ovens, and construction materials. They, too, pump new money into manufacturing.

And when it comes to job creation, give the U.S. more service companies. According to BLS figures, the service industries are almost totally responsible for the creation of new jobs which sop up the substantial increases in the size of the labor force. And three-fourths of these jobs are in the highest-paying occupational categories—executive, administrative, and professional; engineers and scientists; and technologists and technicians.

BLS projects that these three categories will grow at a "faster than average" or "much faster than average" pace through 1995. Those statistics cast an exceptionally encouraging light on your job outlook and that for displaced managers. The commissioner of the Bureau of Labor Statistics states, "This projected strong growth . . . will make it easier for college-educated workers to find the kinds of employment they want."

MAD AS HELL, AND NOT GOING TO TAKE IT ANYMORE

Some years ago those words by the fed-up anchorman in the famous film *Network* became a clarion call for everyone whose frustrations on the job had reached the breaking point. Now it's reviving as a rallying cry for displaced, threatened, and underutilized middle mangers. They are spurred on by the outrage voiced by all segments of society to the media, to pollsters, and even to members of Congress in their hearing halls. They've focused on hostile takeovers financed by persons who've since confessed in court that they're neither magicians nor geniuses but are playing the game with a marked deck.

They target arrogant executives who pay themselves millions in salaries and *increased* bonuses and perks. One such executive had the nerve to accept a bonus that nearly equaled his company's losses. In the early stages of downsizing, when the wrecking crews dismantled their jobs, managers accepted quietly. They feared retaliation. Recently they've been raising the sashes of their windows and bellowing.

Employees have become fed up with the callous disregard displayed for them. One chief executive said, "You can't pull out of assets once you've bought them without losing face. But it's still respectable to dispose of people." That's the kind of arrogance that wins Emmys for TV actor-executives.

What displaced middle managers are finding now is that, once they overcome the initial blows of sudden discharge, they are encountering fewer and fewer problems in sliding behind different desks. Jack Kable says that as his campaign for reemployment progressed, "I began to feel cocky. I realized that some other companies wanted me. I was getting interviews and building my network. Things were going my way."

The same feelings of strength, if not downright cockiness, are permeating the ranks of middle managers, both those who have been discharged and the survivors. James Challenger was emphatic about the outlook for reemployment: "There is no problem." That bald statement may be suspect among those individuals still adrift in the churning wake of the corporate ship which made them walk the plank. It comes from an outplacement consultant who perennially projects optimism for the benefit of his clients.

Yet, optimists like Challenger are not simply selling the fabled lots in Florida which can only be viewed at low tide. Some corporate executives share his opinion about the job outlook for managers. The vice-chairman of a Bell regional holding company says, "The future of middle management is bright. Changes in corporate structure . . . will significantly increase a manager's responsibility and his accountability."

Middle managers are right to be fed up and to be mad as hell. They are right not to put up with being trampled on anymore. As companies feel more strongly the pinch from the shortage of experienced managers, you are better able to assert strongly the values that employers can derive from utilizing your skills. Additionally, as the dust from the downsizing eruptions settles, it's clear that it was the largest companies that hit the panic button. They did the most damage in terms of firing middle managers.

Beneficiaries of these severe shakeouts have been the smaller companies. They have snapped up surplus managers who bring to them sophisticated skills to enhance their growth. Note that the category is *smaller* companies, not small companies or mom-and-pop operations. The *Fortune* 500, after all, cuts off at sales of nearly half a billion. Smaller companies are by many measures large, even the largest in their specific fields. They offer you tremendous employment opportunities.

Ironically, the survivors in the largest companies, after getting over their early fears that they may be next on the hit list, are now more influential, more relied upon, more needed, and consequently more secure. They are becoming more deeply involved in strategic decisions through closer linkage with senior executives—and less vulnerable.

Other straws in the wind portend a brighter outlook for you. For instance, the sun is no longer shining so brightly on Japan, Inc. As its industry matures, it is struggling with the threats that beset the U.S. Its workers seek greater freedom, more opportunity. Highly competitive countries like Korea and others in the Pacific Rim are challenging Japan in the marketplace. Its threat as a competitor is diminishing. That gives new hope to individuals like you and to American industry which, even without Japan's decline, has been improving its competitiveness.

Threats of hostile takeovers are lessening as the insider trading scandals seize headlines. The big Stock Market crash of October '87 has made some targets less appetizing. Legislation (always a two-edged sword) restricting takeovers has been passed by many states. Court decisions upholding the new laws have been rendered. Whether such legislation improves business prospects in the long run remains to be seen. But it does give companies a respite from takeover concerns. It buys them time to concentrate and implement long-term plans. They're more free to spend money on productive, job-creating pursuits rather than defensive measures, legal fees, and servicing debt.

Futurist and author Alvin Toffler commented in BellSouth's annual report upon the current information-age environment and the changes it engenders. Everyone has more information at their disposal. But it gives only fragmentary pictures of the world in which they live and work.

In this environment, Toffler says, "Decision-making becomes more difficult. The acceleration of change forces us to make more decisions about more complex matters in less time. I believe that what we call democracy arose because of the need for help in making decisions and this need explains why we are now seeing a general push to decentralization. By feeding decision-making to the other parts of the system, decentralization reduces the burden on the center. This not only can improve our decisions, it has a democratizing influence because it gives more people a say in how their lives are run."

Middle managers like you are having more say over how their lives are going to be run. That means more than simply sharing partial control over your destinies. It sets an absolute requirement. In order for companies to succeed, they must more fully employ your and other middle managers' skills.

The outlook for middle managers, then, has brightened considerably. Those of you who are in those to-be-favored ranks must grasp firmly the nettles of current employment problems so that they no longer sting.

CHAPTER 8

Options and Opportunities

Making the Right Choice—For You

TRADITIONAL wisdom dictates that middle managers who are threatened with the loss of their jobs or have already suffered that unkindest cut of all have limited options for action. Find a job. Right away. Go to the position/function/industry/area you know best. Grab the first opportunity to get back on the corporate merry-go-round.

Traditional wisdom is wrong. Now is not the time to leap right back into the saddle. Now is the time to take a long, hard look at the career pony you've been riding. It may not be the one you want. There are other options and opportunities out there just waiting to be explored by an intrepid though out-of-work executive.

This chapter doesn't begin to have all the answers for you. Consider it a fire-starter, an idea-sparker. It works in tandem with Chapter 9. Look to the present chapter to develop a general feel for the multiple directions you can ride off into. Look to Chapter 9 for the road map to help you head off on the right expressway.

Before you charge off into the same business-as-usual direction, take a good look at the different paths in this chapter. And start the procedure by taking a good look at yourself.

PREPARING A PERSONAL REPORT CARD

Before you consider any options and opportunities, you need to take a hard look into your wallet and inside your head and your heart. The former is probably clearer, since numbers are usually easier to ferret out than feelings and desires.

You won't find here a financial blueprint for your job search. Rather you'll get help to put your own dollar situation into perspective. That way, when you consider the options and opportunities available to you, you'll be better able to weigh your alternatives judiciously.

In fact, a personal financial analysis does more than give you a set of facts and figures. It sets parameters for your search strategy, so you know approximately how much time you have to restore your earning power before things get tight. Matching current income and expenses can also help psychologically to cushion the depression of firing by emphasizing how much better off you are than you thought.

Look at the bright side first. You're going to save cash out of pocket on commuting, lunches, entertainment, cleaning bills, maybe even taxes and child care. Many expenses you incur in your job search can be written off. And while the money may not be much, don't be too proud to accept unemployment checks.

Six months on the bench may sound like an eternity, but in today's employment climate, it's not. The rule of thumb, many personnel executives say, is one month of looking for each $10,000 in salary. And from ten to twelve months is not unusual in the executive ranks.

One outplacement firm, Swain & Swain, has even promulgated a detailed formula for determining how long a mid-level manager will be out on the streets. Its particular system employs sixty criteria in an attempt to take the guesswork out of estimating. Factors such as situation of client, style, and attitude are weighted by weeks. For example, if you won't relocate, you add weeks to your potential search time. If you're a team player and have extensive professional contacts, you subtract weeks.

Putting a price tag on lifestyle

No matter how long it takes, you need to take a hard look at your immediate financial position. Among the questions you should consider are:

- What is my exact drop in income (past paycheck versus lump-sum or deferred severance)?
- What benefits do I need to keep and what will it cost me to do so? What can I carry over from my last employer and at what price?
- Do I have any capital equipment (boat, third car) that I should consider divesting? Are there any investments that I should consider liquidating?
- If it comes down to it, what borrowing sources (college fund, insurance, family) do I have available?
- What assets do I have that could serve as loan collateral? Any property that can be remortgaged?
- Are there any substantial personal "extras" that we could do without, like club memberships or organizations with annual dues?

To complement these general areas, you'll probably create a sort of personal P&L sheet with what you take in (from severance, dividends, interest, etc.) and what you must expend (mortgage, food, insurance). Even "standard" items should fall under your cost-cutting glare in times like these.

Start by reviewing the big picture. If you're not exactly financially flush, it may be time to tap all the sweat and bucks you've plunged into your house, sell it, and move to less expensive digs. Many older executives who don't have children at home are opting for this strategy. They can then use the sweat equity to set up a business for themselves, invest in one, or establish another source of income.

Less dramatic measures will probably suffice. Review your car insurance. Do you really need collision on the old clunker you used to drive to the train station? Alter some family traditions. A new car every two years, spring clothing sprees, and late summer vacations to Nantucket may have to be put on the back burner. Change some habits. One tune-up a year for the family station wagon instead of two. Regional auto vacation instead of long-distance airplane trip. A barbecue at home instead of dinner with friends in the city.

That's not to say you condemn yourself and your family to living like hermits or monks. Apply the ingenuity you developed on the job to your personal family life. Find substitutes and alternatives. Try regional cultural events and local theatre troupes. Replace a vacation with a family get-together. Lower your sports sights from the high-ticket pros to the less expensive (and often free) college, semipro, and high school level. Don't wait for an Olympic year to become reinterested in alternative sports, gymnastics, ice skating, track.

TURNING YOUR ANALYSIS ON YOURSELF

The dollar dilemma is one quadrant of the overall road map you're sketching. While your financial situation may dictate how fast and how far you can travel in probing options and opportunities, your personal and professional preferences will circumscribe the directions you take. So take time first to figure out where you're coming from and where you really want to go. Ask yourself a series of "insider" questions about the past, present, and future.

Past

- What would you change about your last position if you had to do it over? What part of that previous job did you like most? . . . and least?
- Are there any patterns in your achievements, functions you've excelled in, areas that have brought out the best in you?
- How did you feel about the *type* of your last job?
- What off-job activities have interested you more than past jobs?
- How does what you did stack up against what your peer group is doing?
- What types of people have you found it easiest to work with? . . . and hardest?
- What specifically did you like best when you were twenty to twenty-five, before you got locked into your current profession?

Present

- If you could have someone else's job (let's eliminate Steven Spielberg and Lee Iacocca), whose would you choose?
- What skills or abilities do you have that could be labeled marketable commodities?
- Pick a job, an industry, a profession, and picture yourself in it. How do you look?
- What traits mark your style? Are you a risk taker, a decision maker, a detail person?
- Does office politics turn you off and independence turn you on?

- Do you have a personal definition of success and a series of achievable goals?

Future

- What do you think you want to be doing five years from now (besides not pounding the pavement looking for a job!)?

A ton of tests have been developed to tell you what you are cut out to do. (You'll even see a few quiz questions in Chapter 11 on building your own business.) What it basically comes down to is some serious introspection and systematic reevaluation on your part to determine the real business you.

In the next chapter you'll see some of the nuts and bolts of researching particular jobs, industries, regions, and other considerations. But put away the tool kit for a minute. Before you look at the specifics of looking, you should consider some general avenues that are open to you in your job-hunting decision making. Crucial to a successful outcome—don't limit your search to only what you've done in the past. Push back your horizons and let your imagination wander through some of these options.

SMALL IS BEAUTIFUL

"The overwhelming majority of managers I counsel want nothing to do with big companies once they've been dumped," claims Donald Sweet, who formerly toiled for Costello, Erdlen and now is associated with Hawkins Associates in Summit, New Jersey. "They've been through the mill at those giants, and the feeling is that all big companies are the same—unfeeling, disloyal, arrogant."

Arthur Zelvin, president of the graphics design firm Shareholder Reports, wants to know how to get his hands on a few of those stellar managers being tossed overboard by the major corporations. His contention is that smaller growing companies are fertile grounds for such jettisoned managers, and the marriage of the two would be ideal for both sides.

If you're determined to dive back into the corporate waters, consider targeting a pond as opposed to an ocean. All statistics point to high growth potential in smaller-size firms (and remember size is relative—after all, there are only 500 *Fortune* 500 firms!). Those smaller firms, especially in industries like financial services and high-tech, are looking to fill management positions right up to and including CEOs and COOs.

Before you go charging in that direction, be aware that small doesn't mean easy. Said one observer: ". . . if you're looking at smaller firms, you've got to claw positions out of rock with your bare hands sometimes. And then you may still lose your grip."

Especially if you've always worked for a larger corporation it's a good idea to mull over the advantages of "going small" before you decide what size company to target. Among them are:

- More variety in responsibilities and projects
- Less office politics and fewer layers of bureaucracy
- A more energetic environment, more dynamic personal interaction
- Increased sense of individual involvement
- Greater opportunities to make meaningful contributions
- A shorter chain of command, more responsiveness

CHOOSING THE COUSIN-CAREER ROUTE

If you can't be enticed into the embrace of a smaller firm, you can still return to the corporate fold without heading through the same old position chute through which you exited. Most fired executives don't want to confront career change. So call it redirection instead.

You're looking for jobs in the general area where your management training has been, but not necessarily in the specific functional niche you've always inhabited. The job may be a kissing cousin (e.g., you're an accountant and you slide over into finance), or it may be a position related by marriage (you've managed a DP group and now must supervise within an MIS department).

At the same time, keep an eye out and an ear open for the "needs" of your industry, profession, function, not just within your firm. Listen to what colleagues, superiors, and industry leaders are labeling needs or trends or future areas of potential. Is there a service or product you can offer to satisfy? How about starting a trade publication or an information outlet for a slice of your industry? Or setting up a recruitment agency to specialize in what you've been specializing in all along?

You may have to consider what the buzzword creators have termed career bridging. Especially in such turbulent times in middle management, that perfect job may be as elusive as the Jewel of the Nile. It may be hard to reach in one job-search leap. So take two. Consider a job that will at least propel you in the proper direction (and may even surprise you by being more interesting than you expected). For example, while the service sector may be your final goal, you may want to take advantage of a skill-expanding position in an industrial firm, should it come along.

THE BIGGEST HIRING MACHINE

Maybe you'll decide that private industry just isn't your cup of tea. In that case you should consider America's largest employer—Uncle Sam. The usual executive stream runs from government into the private sector. So buck the trend. Investigate public-sector jobs at local, regional, state, and federal levels.

In some cases civil service requirements, now administered by the Office of Personnel Management, may prove a deterrent to your aims. So start with OPM and check it out. Research that federal job market. Don't overlook town and city government offices. Ask about federal employers located outside Washington, D.C. Be alert to major reorganizations of agencies or government departments.

Check back into your personal fact file. Did you ever deal with a government agency on a project? Are there sectors of the government with close ties to your industry? Have you ever been involved with one of the octopus agencies with tentacles everywhere, like the Office of Management and Budget or even the ubiquitous Defense Department?

And while you're at it, think about unions as well. So what if your only contact has been on the other side of a negotiating table. Maybe a union could use your fresh perspective on its negotiating team. Or you could apply your talents at an administrative level. Look into it. You may be pleasantly surprised.

Even a foreigner might have a spot for you. That doesn't mean you'll have to pull up stakes and sail the ocean blue. What it does mean is that foreign companies are carving out a place for themselves in the American corporate jungle. They need managers who know American business. They may need you.

More and more foreign companies are pumping more and more money into the American economy via investments, acquisitions, joint ventures, plant openings, etc. Those non-U.S. firms will need help. Could you use your skills to serve as a liaison/consultant between them and their U.S. partners or targets to help ease the transition? Or maybe your knowledge of the U.S. market will prove valuable to an overseas company looking to establish a beachhead. Just who were your foreign competitors at your last job?

Don't automatically reject the option of working abroad either. Many large companies make an overseas assignment an offer that can't be refused by their managers. Even management recruiters are establishing closer ties with overseas affiliates. While most searchers are looking for nationals for their clients, you never know.

Several big-time recruiters, including Egon Zehnder, Spencer Stuart & Associates, and Korn-Ferry International have substantial overseas ties. Korn-Ferry even collects and disseminates overseas executive employment intelligence. According to its research, for example, demand for senior executives rose dramatically in one recent year. The hot spots included Japan, Switzerland, the U.K., the Benelux countries, and Australia, while the soft spots were Hong Kong, Malaysia, Singapore, Mexico and Latin America.

GOING BACK TO SCHOOL

Too old for the halls of academia, you lament. You can't teach an old dog to teach, you paraphrase. You're wrong, according to the growing stream of business people becoming teachers. Dust off your diploma and take a look behind the ivy-covered walls as a potential place of employment.

Consider some of the benefits. A teaching position will enable you to utilize your maturity and life experiences to enrich the lives of others. You'll make a positive contribution to society and maybe a difference in the lives of certain individuals. You can use your organization skills and training expertise to advantage. And you can test your mettle in a new setting with a different set of challenges. Further, the personal trauma of losing your corporate job may be eased by a less competitive atmosphere in many teaching assignments, and you'll usually have a more familial orientation to replace the dog-eat-dog circumstances of the business workplace.

While the pay certainly won't be as good, you'll enjoy benefits like group life and health insurance, potential to achieve another pension, and extended periods of free time (summer, holiday schedules) when you can augment your income and take advantage of consulting opportunities.

You could start off by serving as a part-time faculty member for an evening MBA program at your local college or university. Teach your business specialty. The academic community eats up hands-on experience. You can graduate from there if you find you and teaching make the grade together. A number of companies and universities have developed programs to help solve the double dilemma of too few teachers and too many out-of-work managers.

When Chevron announced its plans to cut the work force 15 percent, it also heralded the start of its EN-CORE program. This offers early retirees a chance to retrain and begin new careers in public schools as math or science teachers. Special counseling/training programs were set up at San Francisco State, the University of Houston, and the University of New Orleans. The company, institution, and manager each pick up a piece of the cost. Depending on the circumstances, in eighteen months ex-employees can obtain a teaching certificate in such subjects as math, science, English, and foreign languages.

Other colleges and universities have thrown their hats in the middle manager retraining ring as well. Arizona State started a program for mid-life military retirees, but it became so popular, the school expanded it to include others.

Fairleigh Dickinson University in New Jersey has established a model graduate program in its School of Education called Second Career Alternatives in Teaching for Scientists (SCATS). It is designed to attract and retrain industrial mid-life scientists and technical professionals for new careers as teachers.

At Washington University in St. Louis, middle managers with a B.A. degree can take an intensive thirty-hour program in data processing that equips them to handle the job responsibilities of an MIS professional. And the Academy of Food Marketing at St. Joseph's University in Philadelphia encourages older managers to take its courses in management for food and allied industries. Such courses could be a welcome enhancement of your current skills and might propel you into a combination field you might not otherwise have considered.

ME, A TEMPORARY? FORGET IT!

That's the most likely reaction of an unemployed manager—and a major reason why this is an underexploited option for terminated types. Most haven't even considered it. Do.

The numbers don't lie. According to the Bureau of Labor Statistics, the number of employees whose primary income comes from temp work doubled in the last three years. Industry experts expect employment for top-level temporaries to grow 5 percent per year for the next few years. The medical and legal professions are on the cutting edge of this trend, but the boom is swelling in other professions, like finance and accounting, as well.

Once you've disabused yourself of the old-fashioned notion that a temporary position requires a skirt, pleasant phone manner, and typing skills, you can take an objective look at whether this may be an employment opportunity for you to explore. Or you may cling to out-moded beliefs and be forced by economic circumstances to tap other sources. Like the insurance middle manager who drove a cab for two days before he "lost his mind." Or the editorial department head who is still fitting shoes at a department store.

If you're looking into "flexible staffing" (a temporary by any other name . . .), know that there are pros and cons to the concept. Harold Mers of the well-known 40 + Club organization calls temporary work the "velvet trap." He claims that a job-seeker should be just that, spending full time and energy on his or her search, not getting deflected or distracted by a temporary job. On the other hand, a financial planner from California counseling an unemployed bank executive recommended that he utilize his DP experience to find work in programming through a temp firm.

If you specify part-time work, you can still pursue your hunt for a better job on your days off. Some top-level temps have embraced the notion wholeheartedly. They work under longer-term "contracts," not daily or even weekly assignments in some cases. They may work by the month, or a specific period every month, or for the length of a project. They are more like the freelance "Lone Rangers" you'll see described later in this chapter.

Many of the same benefits of the freelance life are enjoyed by temp employees. You'll have flexibility in scheduling, variety in projects, extra time off, opportunities to meet new people. In most cases, you'll also get work at the pleasure of the temp service and have to pay for individual insurance and other fringe benefits. But competition in some areas, both geographic and functional, has forced some temp firms to consider offering benefit plans that almost border on the attractive. Some pay for life insurance and offer lower-cost group health, for example.

Once you've decided to explore this option, don't just head to the yellow pages for a trip through the T section. Temporary firms at the level you are looking for specialize, so you want one that concentrates on your business or profession. Check out the same characteristics you'd look for in any supplier—client list, reputation, principals, background, etc.

Temp firms that specialize in upper-level management assignments, which is the direction you're looking, often have technical in their names and are sometimes referred to as employment contractors. To home in on those in your field, check trade publications for advertising, ask contacts in the industry, and investigate associations involved in the temp industry.

For example, *Engineer Weekly* in Kirkland, Washington, has an annual directory. There is the New York Association of Temporary Services. Uniforce has sixty offices in twenty states, and Washington, D.C., is home to Rent-A-Consultant. Accountemps, the big executive search firm, has a program called "executive corner." KRON Medical Corp. is on the East Coast and Lawsmiths on the West.

As you can see, the temporary field is wide open. But perhaps you've been salivating at the thought of finally working for yourself.

TALES OF LONE RANGERS

They don't wear masks, but they do operate under a variety of different names. Freelancer. Part-timer. Contingent worker. These people are related to temporaries in that they are not full-time. They are usually in business for themselves, trying to sell their services to a variety of high bidders. By one estimate, 60 percent of the 23 million net new jobs generated in the U.S. since 1974 were for Lone Ranger types.

Even those downsizing companies who put you in the position you're in now have become a partner to this trend. They call it the two-tier system. Basically it involves utilizing outside resources for formerly in-house activities, especially public relations, lobbying, technical projects, training, even financial activities.

Smaller firms are also able to utilize freelance individuals like the "CFO to Go," savvy financial execs who work for several different firms and whose desks are their briefcases. Prime targets for such freelance efforts are start-ups, high-tech firms, mom-and-pop operations and especially retail and manufacturing organizations. They obtain your expertise and hard work, but don't have to put you on the payroll. Your benefits:

- The freedom of scheduling when you want to work and for whom
- Feeling like you're an essential import rather than a domestic cog, a professional gunslinger called in to set things right
- Variety in assignments, locations, projects and people
- The opportunity to test your skills and the challenge to expand your capabilities
- The chance to test various waters, to informally try out "positions" with different companies in different areas

Make no mistake, it is hard work. Besides having to know your specialty inside and out (a financial rover may be hit with projects from capital financing to pricing structures to bank negotiations), you also have to be a juggler of time and assignments, a consummate salesman to bring in the business, energetic and unflappable in the face of conflicting emergencies, able to prioritize, persuasive without being abrasive—all in all, not a calling for everyone.

If you're eyeing the freelance route to fame and fortune, you also need a few other items like:

- The resources to get you through the inevitable lean periods
- A specified market and the capability to reach it in a cost-effective manner
- Complete confidence in your ability, and the ability to communicate that confidence
- A hook for prospective clients, a unique or fresh approach that sets you apart from the pack
- A method and plan for gaining exposure, for promoting yourself
- Knowledge of what the market will bear in terms of what you can charge and what you have to produce

You can tell that the contingent concept is a force to be reckoned with by the diversity of organizations involved with it. For example, you have the Association of Part-Time Professionals, located in Virginia, offering a newsletter, a guide for obtaining and succeeding at part-time work, a directory of employers in Washington who use part-timers, and even group insurance for its members. Companies are staking claims. Arthur Young, the Big Eight accounting and consulting giant, is setting up an Entrepreneurial Services Department in several cities to provide small firms with discounted services similar to the roving CFO concept. Some management-consulting firms (even outplacement organizations) offer contract service programs where they provide assistance for temporary in-house situations at client firms by supplying their own contract consultants.

Finally, you have the growing wave of terminated executives turning to past employers, former colleagues, old comrades in arms, almost anyone in their networks—as they try to join the legions of the successfully self-employed.

TURNING YOUR HOBBY INTO CASH

It all starts innocently enough. You rewrite a colleague's speech. Teach a couple of secretaries the rudiments of sailing. Make a few speeches on the implications of the new tax reforms. Maybe even sell a couple of watercolors at the local art exhibit. Suddenly it's not so innocent. You've exhibited the first signs of the hobby self-employment fever.

Whatever you do, don't drop either your job search or your regular job if you're lucky enough to still be on the rolls of the employed. If you're contemplating turning that hobby into a living, do some moonlighting first. See if you like working at it as much as you like playing at it.

A lot of people apparently do. By one estimate, ten years ago a paltry 5 percent of fired white-collar and management types turned their hobbies into sources of livelihood. Today that estimate has quadrupled. Not only are there more of the terminated types, but the list of potential hobby fields cum business opportunities is limited only by the imaginations of those pursuing them.

Stories abound. A former hospital personnel director exchanged his white staff coat for a chef's hat, and turned his love for cooking and hatred for commuting into a gourmet hot-dog-stand operation. That life step earned him a ton of publicity and a steady income, and started visions of franchised frank stands sizzling in his head.

An investment banker changed his pinstripes and turned back the clock to childhood for his enterprise. He produces and sells baseball cards featuring portraits of Hall of Fame stars.

The list is endless:

- The entire leisure industry, for those who take their fun and games seriously—managing a club, a hotel, a chain, or overseeing a condominium or resort complex, or teaching an avocation such as tennis or golf
- Physical endeavors—pottery, painting, house restoration, real estate caretaker, dog breeding, wine-grape growing;
- Mental jobs—ghostwriting, editing, teaching language to adults, guest lecturing on formal gardens

As with all business matters, this area too has its own buzzword—"midpreneur." That kind of individual takes a hobby and turns it into a moneymaking venture.

A warning: as in all business, it's a tough row to hoe. Trying to turn an avocation into a vocation is a calculated risk and a special challenge. It's certainly not all sweetness and light and childhood dreams. Besides all the normal problems surrounding starting your own business (see Chapter 11 and remember the estimates that four of five new businesses fail in the first few years), you also have special tax considerations. They can hamstring you.

So there you have it—a laundry list of major thoroughfares to explore in your attempt to put your career back on track to success. Do you become a temp? Strike out as a Lone Ranger? Or will you opt to buy or build a business of your own? Whatever your initial leaning is, don't fall into any decision before you learn more of the specifics of the job search.

CHAPTER 9

Successful
Job Searches

Keeping the Faith
While You're Pounding
the Pavement

THIS chapter isn't designed to help you go out tomorrow morning and find your dream job. Although it may, in fact, propel you in that direction. It is meant to help you write your own ticket to career change with a maximum of control and direction, by complementing the general strategies available to help you make the right choice with specific tactics and techniques to implement.

If you want to learn how to write a better résumé, or act more composed in an interview, or look more like Lee Iacocca in front of millions, well, there is an Empire State Building stack of books on the market that will try to teach you those things. The following messages are as much psychological as practical. They say: "Here are specific aspects of a job search from a strategic perspective. Combine them with the big-picture alternatives from the last chapter when you're trying to put together your personal game plan for getting your career back on track."

If just one idea from this chapter makes your job search faster, easier, more successful then it has done its job.

Best approaches to successful job searches

Plain old dumb luck might take the number-one spot if you were to conduct a survey of what most job-finders attributed their success to. And probably just as often you'd hear "sheer hard work." But if you dig a little deeper, you'll find certain other themes repeat themselves in successful searches.

Discipline. "Very few individuals have it in the amounts necessary to conduct a focused search," said one personnel consultant. The process of looking involves taking a whole lot of baby steps, each one planned to follow the next. Those who just dive in headfirst are likely to find themselves smacking into the bottom of an empty pool.

Refuse to be discouraged. One headhunter estimates it will take a manager, on average, 1,100 résumés and 2,100 calls to land a job. Another has a somewhat more sanguine view—600 to 900 contacts. No matter what it takes, the ultimately successful searcher never lets discouragement get the upper hand. "It's funny," said one ex-looker. "I saw job ads that I was perfect for. Perfect. But I never even got a nibble." You must be able to rebound from such discouraging situations.

Take it all in stride. This related requirement for equanimity comes in handy when you are treated, as one discharged executive put it, "like a goddamned leper." Whatever you do, don't wander into the fray feeling like nobody wants you and that you can't succeed. That attitude will become a self-fulfilling prophecy.

Set a system. It may be purely your own, and it may skip steps that even this book recommends. But you must create one, monitor it, make sure it's working. Get an outside opinion on how you're progressing in your search. At the very least, take your own "search pulse" regularly. Are your objectives still viable? Your target audience still appropriate? Your salary expectations still realistic? Your résumé and interview manner compelling? In short, would you hire you?

Ride the rollercoaster. In the heat of the search, your emotions will escalate to exhilaration and plummet to depression with practically every ring of the telephone or tap of the mailman's steps. You see a job that fits you to a T, have a great interview, and then get shot down by a "Dear John" letter. All the great athletes advise: "Don't let yourself get too high or too low. Perform on a consistent level." Good advice.

Specifically, network. A poor résumé will hurt. And lack of interview polish is a drawback. But an outplacement axiom says it all. "Network, or not work." Conversely, the number-one culprit of failed job searches is often fingered as not networking correctly—or at all.

There are several other common ways in which job candidates either shoot themselves in the foot during their search or stick that foot in their mouths. Among the prime irritants for employers, personnel interviewers, and even executive recruiters are:

- Canned résumés and cookie-cutter cover letters
- Inadequate homework
- Negative attitudes (know it all, critic, bad-mouther)
- Lack of attention to appearance
- Dull as dishwater job history listed strictly chronologically

A job search also bucks the odds for success when the candidate works a short search week, severely limits his or her options by geography, commute time, company size, or doesn't employ the myriad resources available for a search. But before utilizing the weapons, you should get an idea of where you plan to squeeze off your shots.

THE OUTLOOK FOR LOOKING

Doing a little detective work can make all the difference in eventually finding the right targets to focus your job search on. And those targets don't just include specific companies or positions. Always keep your eyes and ears open, whether employed or not, for a wide variety of trends, statistics, and projections that may have an impact on where and how you look.

Remember the days when you were too busy to look at those magazines with their "annual issues" of the fastest-growing, most-admired, best-run companies? And you passed right over the industry growth projections in the newspaper to get to the sports section? And who cares about where the U.S. Bureau of Labor Statistics (BLS) says employment is looking up?

Well you care. At least you should. That's not to say your entire job search strategy will hang on what your research finds. But every little bit helps—to give you a feel for where you should aim your hunting arrows, what professional directions may be most fruitful, what business and personal opportunities are opening up, and which are closing. And importantly, it gives you a psychological edge, a confidence in the fact that your search is better researched, better planned, better orchestrated—to get you a better job.

Take magazines, for instance. If you're looking for small-company opportunities, you should check out the *Business Week* ranking of the best small growth companies, including the city in which they are headquartered. *Forbes* compiles a top-200 honor roll for small companies, and even includes CEO names, headquarters addresses, and telephone numbers.

Forbes also publishes an annual report card on American industry with financial ratings on companies, designations of the most improved, and even some tips on job prospects. It points out something you may not have included in your prospective target calculations; namely that seemingly desirable cities like Phoenix, San Diego, and San Antonio have a double whammy for job searchers. They are submerged by waves of retirees who want to keep working and military personnel completing service and vying for private sector jobs.

Projections abound on how cities stack up as growth areas and targets for job hunts. *Fortune,* in early 1987, published predictions of job prospects for metro areas in the 1990s. Los Angeles is expected to top New York as the number-one job center in the country, Boston is a comer, and even Amherst near Buffalo is identified as a boom town in the rust belt. *Fortune* also throws in a little tidbit concerning "corridor booms." For example, in New Jersey half of the most recent growth in private employment occurred along major highways.

Inc. magazine has gotten into the act with lists of the fifty fastest-growing cities, citing new start-up companies, high-growth organizations, and overall increases in employment. The point is not that you memorize these cities and plan to move where opportunities seem the most wide open. Instead, all these considerations, trends, ideas should be fed into your personal job search "database" for background.

Here are a few more bon mots to tuck away:

- The BLS says Florida and Georgia are particularly robust in the "managers and officials" employment category; the energy states have been sapped by the woes of the oil patch, and employment is staggering there; unemployment figures for the Northeast are the lowest in the nation.

- Hot cities according to most reports are Austin, Orlando, Atlanta, and Boston; not so hot are Peoria, Huntington, West Virginia, and Davenport, Iowa. Housing is most affordable in St. Louis, Cleveland, Indianapolis, and Kansas City (sounds like a list of NFL have-nots), and least affordable in New York, San Diego, Denver (did someone say Super Bowl?).

- When ranked by per capita tax burden and income tax rates, Washington, D.C. (not suprisingly), leads the pack, followed by New York State, Wyoming, and Minnesota, with Tennessee, Kentucky, and Arkansas bringing up the rear.
- Korn-Ferry, the executive-recruitment and consulting firm, dispatches quarterly updates on job prospects; one release reported that a surge in demand had hit for senior managers in financial services, high tech, international marketing, hospitality and leisure, and even the public sector on the state and local level.

KEEPING YOUR CRYSTAL BALL IN FOCUS

Now to the nitty-gritty: What industries, professions, and companies offer the greatest job potential? Again, consider this an awareness exercise, adding more building blocks to your search structure.

You may say, "I'm staying put. The only industry I want to know about is the one I've been in." The last chapter on options and opportunities should have made you want to rip off those blinders and check out what's slightly beyond your normal target range.

The hot spots are in the headlines all the time. You just have to know how to decipher them. Take financial services for example. Mostly you read about the insider trading scandals and the perils of the Ivan Boeskys of the world. At the same time, the BLS is projecting a 17-percent job growth rate in the financial services field by 1990, with 280,000 positions in management. Said one executive-search specialist: "There's a tremendous shortage of managers in financial services . . . and the boom won't end for five years." Then you have the growing trend toward internationalism in financial markets with their inherent time differentials. That has created need for twenty-four-hour operations, and thus an extra helping of managers to oversee those "graveyard shifts" on the market floor. Some experts claim the turmoil caused by the October '87 Stock Market crash has re-emphasized the need for experienced and down-to-earth managers.

What about other emerging growth areas where your management expertise and experience may be welcome, areas as diverse as robotics, biotechnology, services to the retired, hazardous-waste industry, and telemarketing in television? Research them. And don't concentrate only on the high profiles. Check out the high-turnover sectors too.

Listen to what the industry leaders are saying. The executive director of the Association of Field Service Managers (computers and other office communications equipment) claims that industry revenues will grow 14 percent annually through 1990 and the industry already employs 27,000 managers whose ranks will increase 2–3 percent per year. Or Korn-Ferry again, whose National Index of Executive Vacancies pinpoints financial services and accounting as hot-ticket professions, followed by health care, high tech and consumer products.

Don't overlook the uncommon professions that garner little press ink and almost no discussion. Could your skills be sold in such small niches as:

- An urban geographer, a/k/a market researcher, usually involved in real estate, examining demographic patterns to assess market potential
- A technology investigator, similar to what companies like Exxon and General Electric do to keep up with the competition; you read technical magazines, attend conferences, review "white papers" and use creative intelligence to tie trends and opportunities to potential plans and strategies
- A knowledge engineer who conducts in-depth interviews of experts, not for their knowledge, but to

analyze their thought processes (e.g., in decision making) in order to convert those processes into a computer program

- A data security manager who oversees a program of protection for corporate information (colleges like St. John's University in New York now offer a course in this field)
- A corporate ethics trainer/consultant, since the subject is in all the headlines today and will probably touch bottom lines tomorrow; it's in vogue to have corporate culture include an ethical-behavior slant and to have employees learn how to handle touchy ethical situations

The point is, don't be afraid to look in unexplored places for interesting positions. They're out there.

DEVISING A PERSONAL STRATEGY

At the same time you're looking outside to lay the groundwork for your job search, take some time to look inside as well. You need a personal strategy for selling yourself that exploits your strengths and negates your weaknesses. Before you get into the action aspects of your search, with networks, résumés, and the like, you should put together a specific game plan that you want to follow. Get your game face on.

Turn your age to advantage. Many employers see gray hair on a job candidate and immediately begin to count the downsides. They may think you're so set in your ways that you're hard to manage; or that you're exceptional and will threaten the security of their own position; or you're slowing down with age, or being passed by, losing a step; or—the list is endless.

Prepare an aggressive response to that attitude. If you sense you're being compared unfavorably to the generic "younger manager," give actual examples from your experience showing that:

- You're more committed, reliable, dedicated
- Your work ethic is stronger
- You provide a fresh perspective
- Your ideas and innovations are based on proven systems
- You'll make fewer mistakes and take less training to get up to speed

Stick to your strategy. Once you've completed your homework and launched your campaign, don't deviate. Keep forging ahead no matter how many roadblocks you encounter. You might be forced to sidestep slightly, but keep your eyes focused on the goal line. Monitor your system, making sure you're in control and following your game plan.

Explore new tactics. Don't be constrained by the programs you're given in outplacement (see Chapter 10) or by a recruiter's advice or by what you read in the self-help books. Seize any and all opportunities to expand the boundaries of your job search. Go to conventions and luncheons at your own expense and on your own initiative. Strike up conversations with speakers, moderators, anyone with contacts. Your motto should be "I will be visible."

Consider a "contrarian strategy." Instead of looking for fast-growth companies, check out companies that are floundering. Your talents may be more appreciated there. You'll have a chance to test your mettle quicker, have more room to strut your stuff. If—or rather when—you start to shine, that beacon will light a new path for career success.

Finally, play the field, the whole field. Don't be afraid to go after anything that piques your interest. An out-

of-work marketing executive misread a classified ad. After
spending a lot of interviewing time finding out he wasn't
in the ballpark, he was naturally discouraged, but un-
daunted. So he asked a friend to inquire about the job
and put in a good word for him. The employer eventually expanded the job requirements. And it hired the
marketer for a position with national scope and pay substantially higher than his former one. All because he
misread an ad but refused to quit.

PLAYING THE NETWORKING GAME

Besides misreading the ad, the executive did one other
thing that every person in the field says is crucial for
job-search success. The single most emphatic piece of advice was to get out there and establish a network, whether
you're still in a job, are looking for a new one, or have
just found one. Said one newly hired former job searcher:
"Security is not only being good at what you do. It's being
good at networking." Said another: "The best advice I
can give anyone in any position in business today is to
build a network. Be a joiner, an activist. Even if it turns
into a pain in the ass. It's not wasted."

That joining aspect of networking was underlined by
a number of counselors. The opportunities are varied,
from your local Republican or Democratic committees to
professional trade associations to college advisory boards
to community volunteer organizations. Also be on the
lookout for company alumni associations. You may even
consider starting one with the other members of your
organization who were swept out in the same termination whirlwind with you.

Procter & Gamble and General Electric are two giants
which have spawned associations of ex-employees who
keep in touch. Xerox has its "X-Group" of over 1,200
strong. The Time-Life Alumni Society has a directory of

more than 1,000 members. This organization gets unusually strong corporate support, including cut-rate subscriptions to publications and an office at company headquarters.

Also keep in touch with those colleagues and associates you left behind who are still toiling in the vineyards. Ties to former cronies are often the most fruitful and should be nurtured systematically. Use a little psychology on them—and yourself. Most managers say they are embarrassed to call an old comrade in arms for help in troubled times. They feel a stigma about being fired, as if someone emblazoned a scarlet F on their chests for all to see. "Bull-dingey," as Colonel Potter of *M*A*S*H* would say.

Turn that attitude around. You're doing a favor for all those individuals you draw into your search network, not only former colleagues but other contacts as well. Why? For one thing, people like to help other people. For another, you'll make them feel important. You go to them for their sage advice and counsel. Their hat sizes will surely expand. Remember, when you do well in your next job, it will offer reflected glory to the former colleague who recommended you.

Also, you put yourself in their debt. You "owe them one." If they never collect, they feel one up. Those still back at the office might even feel pangs of guilt. "There but for the grace of God go I." So giving them a chance to help you can assuage some of their own negative feelings.

And finally, they'll certainly be pleased to have you finally find work. It'll be a load off their minds, and maybe their backs.

There's no limit to the number, sizes, and shapes of network contacts. You may nod your head in assent, but then do what most job searchers do: limit your network to only the most obvious candidates. Donald Sweet, the experienced outplacement consultant for Hawkins Associates, tells a few "stranger than true" stories that might start you thinking along less limiting lines. In an interview, he recounted:

"I called my dentist with an emergency one Saturday morning. I begged him to give up his golf game or whatever and work on my tooth. He agreed—with one stipulation. I had to review a résumé and give some advice to an unemployed friend of his. That really impressed me, that this networker had drafted his own dentist into the ranks.

"Then there's the story about the gas station attendant who noticed a pile of résumés on the back seat of a regular customer's car. When the guy told the attendant he had been fired, the latter asked for several copies. The result: two interviews. Same happened in an offshoot of the merry mailman routine. Guy was home mowing his lawn after being sacked. Mailman strolled by and asked if he was on vacation. When he heard of the ex-manager's plight, he took a couple of résumés and stuffed them in mail boxes of executives he knew down the block. Result: more interviews.

"One of the most convoluted I ever heard involved a woman who dragged herself up to a vegetable vendor's stand with a hangdog expression on her face. She was very upset because her husband had lost his job, she explained. Well, it turned out the vendor had a lawn service on the side, and one of his clients was a big-wheel executive. Want to guess what happened next?

"One of the best is about a fellow who was unceremoniously dumped just two days after his twenty-fifth anniversary celebration with the firm, gold watch and all. He was a very religious person and active in the community, so everyone knew and liked him. The next Sunday in church, his pastor gets up for his sermon and announces that one of the congregation is in need of help. Think about it. What better place to put the arm on someone for a job than from the pulpit!"

The point is not to go out and plaster your résumé

on every street corner. It is, though, never to pass up the opportunity to network—with anyone. They don't have to be movers and shakers to be helpful. Take a long look at the following short list.

Personal

Neighbors
Clients
Friends
Acquaintances

Old Job

Competitors
Peers
Bosses
Clients
Employees
Salespeople
Suppliers
Customers

Church

Officers
Members
Sunday-school teachers
Ushers

Outside Activities

Sports associates (golf, tennis, bowling)
Club members
Association contacts
Trade organizations

Community

Volunteer groups
Chamber of Commerce

United Fund
Kiwanis
Scouts
Lodge brothers
PTA

Family

Father, mother
Brother, sister
In-laws
Cousins, uncles, aunts

Other Professionals

Lawyers
Accountants
Doctors/dentists
Bankers
Investment counselors

School

Professors
Officials (dean, etc.)
Sorority
Fraternity
Classmates
Other alumni

Other

Public officials
County leaders
Political-club members
Military
Children's friends'
    parents

DO'S AND DON'TS
OF NETWORKING

The job seeker Don Sweet spoke about may have suffered an initial bout of embarrassment when his plight was "broadcast" from the church steeple, so to speak. But one of the prime requirements for successful networking is "don't be embarrassed." There are several others.

Don't get discouraged. Some people get bent out of shape when their phone calls aren't returned or promises go unkept. Brush-offs are like brush-back pitches in baseball. You haul yourself up, dust yourself off, and step back into the contest more determined than ever to hit a homer.

Do send all your contacts, no matter how close, a résumé and cover letter. Refresh their memories about your business accomplishments. You may even jolt a new network contact from their subconscious when they see your material.

Don't turn a network meeting into a job interview. Sure you want to meet and talk with as many spokes in your network wheel as possible. But it's critical that you make it appear that you aren't asking for an audience in order to give them a snow job or beg for a position. Relieve any pressure by assuring the networkee you only seek advice and counsel.

Do keep in regular contact with anyone who responds to your network efforts. People like to hear about progress. Keep them interested and involved in your search with periodic updates. Plus, keep your situation in front of them in case something pops up that they weren't aware of. And if you let them share in the elation of a job found, you'll cement that relationship just in case—heaven forbid!—you ever find yourself in need again.

Do get referrals. Ask if you can use the person's name before you do, even if you must use the term "mutual acquaintance" instead of "friend" when you introduce yourself. Every name counts.

If you ever get discouraged, embarrassed, and downright sick and tired of the whole networking chore, remember the outplacement axiom: NETWORK or NOT WORK.

While networking may help you get your foot in the door, your tongue is your best weapon for actually landing the job. As an organized executive, you should not have trouble doing the practical homework necessary for successful interviewing. You're well trained in analyzing company markets, needs, problems, structures, and other essential criteria. But are you psychologically prepared to match wits with tough interviewers and come away with their respect, admiration—and a job offer?

You know what each potential employer is looking for in terms of the open position from reading the ads, or a preliminary conversation with networkers or even with the interviewer when you make the appointment. But what are employers really looking for?

They've been asked that question ad nauseum over the years by pollsters and researchers. You can gain an interviewing edge by knowing what they've said. For example, here are some common themes that pop up frequently as desirable characteristics/skills/traits from the employer's perspective:

- Appearance of compatability with organization
- Understanding of company problems *and* opportunities
- Well-honed sense of judgment
- Strong analytical tendencies
- Broad information/communication skills
- Higher levels of education and business training
- Sense of value and commitment
- Drive and motivation fired by personal desire to succeed

In job hunting you need to learn how to reflect those desirable aspects with your own experience, background, makeup, and achievements. How can you best translate what you are and what you've done into a presentation that says "I possess all these attributes—creativity, ingenuity, imagination, leadership, energy, work ethic, awareness, savvy, sense of humor, sensitivity, a hands-on shirt-sleeve approach to problem solving—and more."

You've got to become the candidate that the interviewer is looking for without pretending or putting on airs. You develop yourself to reveal the key elements of your own personality that fit the bill from the employer's point of view. Remember that interviewer is not there to hire *you*. He or she is there to hire the *person they have in mind for the job*. Your mission is to make sure you are that person.

TAKING THE OFFENSIVE WITHOUT OFFENDING

While you're mentally preparing yourself for the rigors of interviewing, think negative. Then turn it positive. Say you get someone who learned interview techniques by reading about the Spanish Inquisition. You know the type. Keeps you waiting. Offers a dead-fish handshake. Never looks you in the eye. Skips the small talk and immediately throws you a curve. Asks questions like: What was your biggest failure at your last job? What's your major weakness in handling people? What bad things have you heard about this company? If you're so talented, how come you're out of work?

When you go into such an interview cold, your first impulse might be to reach across the desk and rearrange a few facial features on this particular interviewer. But get someone to play such a devil's advocate part beforehand, and you'll retain your composure and have your answers ready.

You can explain how you turned a snafu at your previous company into a positive learning experience for yourself and a future preventive measure for your firm. You can reply that the worst thing you've heard about this potential employer is how tough it is to get a job there. You can be prepared to discuss exactly why a skillful manager like yourself happens to have suffered the slings and arrows of outrageous business fortune in today's tumultuous economy.

You'll also run into the overqualified syndrome. Some seekers are content to have their egos massaged by being told that they're too good. Question: do you want the job or not? Presumably since you took the time to interview, you do. Prepare to fight the "OQ" reaction. There are lots of tacks to take:

"You say I'm overqualified? To do what? To perform this job effectively and proficiently with knowledge and experience built up over the years? To bring to the job superior abilities and skills that should insure excellent performance?"

OR

"Suppose you were utilizing the services of an attorney or an investment analyst or a personal doctor. Would you refuse professionals like that because they were overqualified?"

OR

"I've always felt that the best way to insure my own managerial success was to surround myself with the best people possible, overqualified or not. Don't you agree?"

OR

"You say I may not be happy or satisfied or challenged enough by this new position. Well I sure as hell am not happy or satisfied or challenged by unemployment."

Résumés as interview generators

When you're pounding the pavement and pounding on doors in your job search, a résumé is a requisite. Your local library shelves are laden with a ton of material on the ins and outs of résumé writing. In fact, the plethora of advice creates problems. Whose advice do you follow? Do you type or typeset? One page or two? Chronological order or list of accomplishments?

In the end, you'll have to decide what is best for your particular situation, the target you're aiming at, the position you're hoping for. Some "experts" even disagree as to whether you should tailor a résumé to specific people and organizations, especially in light of the advantages of a personal computer.

As you're creating your own interview generator, though, keep in mind some general guidelines that can make your résumé preparation more productive:

Brief is better. One page if possible, two tops. Keep in mind that the cover (which is mandatory) sells the sizzle, the résumé provides the steak. Spend some extra time on the sizzle.

Slick is out. Colored paper, outsized envelopes, and fancy graphics may call *unwanted* attention. Another "out" that used to be "in" is the "Here's what I can do for you" strategy. Overuse has blunted its effectiveness. Use it as a theme, not as a statement.

Be careful with words. Some generate negative reactions. "Administrative" sounds lower-level than "executive." HRD sounds more modern than "Personnel." And even if you took a sweet early retirement offer, don't use the word retirement. Use "new career opportunities" or something more positive.

Consider a "nonrésumé" résumé. Keep a standard one on hand, but send out an accomplishment report card: your five most significant achievements, what you did and how you did it and why you could give an encore performance at the new job.

Now you're all dressed up in your best résumé and interviewing finery, but where do you go to dance? Besides networking, the prime sources for matchmaking are display ads. (Do not overlook the classifieds.) While combing the "help wanted" columns may not be your idea of pleasant Sunday morning reading, it's another logical, productive step in your search for work.

While you're picking and choosing, don't be overly picky or choosy. Remember the story of the marketing executive who misread an ad and ended up getting a higher-level position. Besides those "perfect" ads, don't ignore the ones for which you may be just a tad over- or underqualified. There may be flexibility in the position.

Also be aware of the ripple effect. If there's a big ad for a certain position, perhaps there is a concurrent need for support functions. If a company is looking for a manager for a new plant, will it need a comptroller for the organization? Accounting help? Whether you're looking for full-time work or freelance, it may be worth an inquiry.

Make the ads part of your strategic search program. Read a lot of them so you "speak their language." Tie the qualifications in your cover letter and résumé to those in the ad. Pick an opportune time to reply to an ad, after the first wave has broken on the potential employer's desk. Address yourself to the functional person, not Personnel, whenever possible.

Ads aren't the only sources you should be using to facilitate your job search. In fact, if you skip straight to the classifieds, you may be overlooking a wealth of opportunities right there in the business pages. The headline won't read "Job opening at XYZ Corp." But it might refer to a resignation, promotion, transfer, retirement, or even, yes, termination. Or the article could be about new products or services, facility expansion, industry developments. Use your analytical skills to extrapolate your own opportunities by reading between the lines.

Look for relocations news, new company underwrit-

ing offerings, significant events like a government project or even a sports happening like the Goodwill Games
in Seattle in 1989. Even annual reports can alert you to
future job openings when you read them in terms of new
products, markets, projects, and the jobs they'll produce.

During your library research, flip through books that
rate companies and explain their strengths and weaknesses. Learn how to use background data books like
the ones listed below.

Sources for Search

- *National Directory of Addresses and Telephone
  Numbers:* Addresses and telephone numbers of
  business establishments, organizations, and a listing of trade publications
- *Directory of Corporate Affiliations:* Addresses, telephone numbers, sales, number of employees, top
  corporate officers, including geographic index section of thousands of corporations and subsidiaries
- *Dun & Bradstreet Million Dollar Directory:* Businesses, product classifications, sales and key officers; also contains geographic and product classifications index
- *Standard and Poor's Register of Corporations, Directors, and Executives:* Similar to Dun and Bradstreet, plus a brief biographical listing of key corporate officers and directors
- *National Trade and Professional Associations of the
  United States and Canada:* Lists associations, addresses, officers, and a brief history
- Industry-specific publications, like *Polk's Directory*
  (banks) and *Best's Directory* (insurance)
- Directories of executive recruiters, personnel agencies
- *Directory of Directories*

- State directories of manufacturing, industrial, and other firms
- National and regional business publications
- *Standard Marketing Classification* from the Department of Labor.

ORGANIZATIONS THAT HELP YOU LOOK

Books are vital to your job search. So are people. As you'll see in the outplacement chapter, an entire industry has sprung up around the downsizing dilemma. But outplacement firms are just one organizational option for the unemployed.

Self-help groups. HELP WANTED is a good example of people getting together to help each other. Operating in Westchester County, New York, it basically involves workshops for executive, administrative, and managerial types who are out of work. While the group deals in the basics of résumés, interviewing, and so forth, founder Bob Steed underlines its underlying aim when he says it was invented "to help people hold body and soul together after they get fired—especially soul."

"You get tremendous emotional support from the commonality of the group," says Steed. "We reinforce the fact that the fired individual is not alone. We have weekly celebrations for those who find jobs, and those rituals also have an important psychological function. They say 'You too can rise above this bad situation and succeed in your job search like this person did.' "

Such groups are heavy on empathy and stroking, helping people feel they are back in control of their situations, that they have a game plan in place and a team to back them up. They also offer a chance to help others, thus raising self-esteem and imbuing feelings of personal worth in group members.

If you can't find such a group, consider starting your

own. Gather people with the common goal of getting a job. Hold regular debriefing sessions, exchange classified ads, books, gossip. You may receive a double benefit once the group gets going if you generate some local media attention.

On a national scale, you can look into the services of the 40+ Clubs, a not-for-profit, member-operated co-op of unemployed executives, managers, and professionals. Almost fifty years old and operating in sixteen cities from New York to Hawaii to Toronto, 40+ is dedicated to helping members conduct an organized and successful job search.

This no-frills operation has a series of fees ($500 to join, $300 to leave) and demands a personal commitment from its members to help each other. You get extensive counseling, constructive suggestions, use of mail service, plus reference library and computers—all the material necessities for your search. Importantly, you also get a sympathetic peer group to lean on, programs like Job Jury so you can take advantage of the experience of others, and even psychological counseling sessions if you want them.

EXECUTIVE RECRUITERS: LOOKING FOR YOU

If you're lucky enough to have a "headhunter" on your trail, take advantage of it. Usually the clients of executive recruiters or executive search firms indicate they don't want "individuals who are on the beach." If you're unemployed, that's you.

If you deal with an executive search firm, ask the same type of questions you'd ask professional outplacement firms. You want to find out how up-front they are, whether they hide behind a veil of confidentiality when you ask sharp questions, who put them on to you in the first place.

Several associations cover this field and they should be researched as part of your personal databank. One is the National Association of Personnel Consultants. It publishes a directory with more than 1,500 firms broken down by certification, by specialty (accounting/finance, legal, marketing), by subcategory (banking, insurance), and by geography. You also get contact names. In 1987, a candidate's edition was published with specific editorial matter for job-seekers.

There are also recruitment networks, from the general (e.g., National Personnel Associates of Grand Rapids) to the specific (e.g., Insurance National Search in Dallas) to major franchise operations like Robert Half Associates. You can also list in computer registration systems that are like huge filing cabinets that an employer can peek into for résumés. Computerized Listings of Employment Opportunities, part of Copley Systems Inc. in California, is representative of this type of operation.

Basically you are looking to cut the time you must invest in looking, increase the number of potential targets and the boundaries of your search, and draw on others' expertise and weapons. But being jobless, you're in a very vulnerable position. Don't let anyone exploit your situation. Approach any professional liaison as a strict business deal.

Be leery of any "career counselor" who claims to have friends in high places—and wants a big hunk of cash up front. Take with a grain of salt any "guarantees" of a job from an agency. In general, the former don't go out and find you a job. Instead they work on your strengths, weaknesses, and interests. So any promise should be taken in context, and all deals should be in the black and white of signed contracts.

You can cover yourself by checking references, professional credentials, the local Better Business Bureau, or even the state's attorney general's office (over a dozen states have filed suits against firms in the career-counseling field), or contacting professional organizations like the National Board of Certified Counselors.

One of the latest pitches from career consultants involves a personalized letter in which they tell you what a great guy or gal you are and that they want to make your job search so very easy. They'll do it all—conduct a soul-searching goal appraisal with you, write your résumé, research your most likely targets, and give you the top 100, make follow-up calls, book interviews, act as confidential message center—all for a mere one month's salary or so from you. It all sounds too good to be true. Often it is, according to some well-publicized horror stories. That doesn't mean you reject career consultants as a factor in your search. It just means that you approach any combination with a weather eye for stormy seas.

Probably the toughest advice to give an unemployed executive looking for a job is "Don't take one." After the trauma of losing your old job and the stress of looking for a new one, when a brass ring appears within your grasp you may be very tempted to grab it without a second thought.

Don't. Yet. First make certain you can be sure about this job, this company, this industry. Have you talked to a colleague who knows the company, or better yet a former executive from that firm? Have you asked about their experiences, how they would characterize management, what the policies are in career development, opportunity to excel, benefits and yes, termination?

Have you looked into the company's financial situation? You certainly don't want to go from the frying pan into the fire. You've just been tossed about in a storm and you need a calm port. You need a corporate climate that fits you and vice versa. Is the company bureaucratic while you tend toward entrepreneurial? Is there a team atmosphere or is it manager-eat-manager? Is a "corporate lifestyle" imposed by top management?

It may be hard to accept, but jumping into a bad situation can put you into a worse pickle than the one you're already trying to resolve with your job search. So make sure before you grab it that the silver platter won't tarnish by the time you get to work tomorrow.

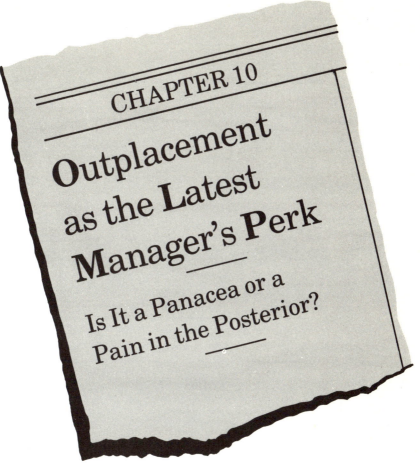

CHAPTER 10

Outplacement as the Latest Manager's Perk

Is It a Panacea or a Pain in the Posterior?

OF all the weapons you can turn to for conducting a successful job search, one of the most modern—and most potent—is outplacement. Utilized correctly, it can help you bag a new and better job in a shorter time frame than you could without it. But like any new concept it has its advocates and its detractors.

"It's just what the doctor ordered," extols one terminated manager. "Just a salve for the corporate conscience," scoffs another. The views of outplacement are as varied as the companies in the business. But one thing is certain: outplacement is a concept whose time has come.

First look at the numbers and status of outplacement consultant (OPC) firms in the U.S., both of which have risen dramatically in recent years. Industry followers claim that since 1982, the number of firms in the field has jumped from about 83 to 130, while revenues for the industry have more than doubled, from $60 million to over $150 million.

Most blue-chip companies today integrate some sort of outplacement help into their dismissal/layoff/retirement programs. A 1985 survey revealed that 80 percent of the *Fortune* 500 provided either internal or external outplacement services. And an increasing number of those recommend specific firms or give their ex-employees lists of potential companies to use.

Outplacement firms generally offer a standard array of services, but often boast specialized programs focused on specific areas, such as video interview preparation, entrepreneurship, or personal counseling. There is also a trend toward specialization by industry and function, à la executive recruiters.

If you're going to get sent to an outplacement firm by your company, why should you want to study the who, what, when, where, and why of the business? Good question. The answer is that outplacement could be the single biggest key to your getting another job, a better job, in the shortest time possible, with the least amount of psychological hassle.

There are other reasons. Your firm may not offer you outplacement services (in which case, consider pushing for it as part of your severance package). If you have to search for an individual outplacement firm—and pay for it—you damn well want to learn everything you can about this booming business so you can jump in feetfirst with eyes open.

Here's another reason. The outplacement firm your company offers you may not be up to snuff. Or the program offered to you may be too short—or too long—or just not suited to you. You may be able to "negotiate up." Or, your company may be following a recent trend and offering you a choice of up to eight or ten companies to use. Then some insights into what's good, bad, and indifferent about firms in this new industry can prove especially valuable.

Whatever your situation turns out to be, know about outplacement. The firm you use can turn into your best friend in a lonely job search.

What is this thing called outplacement?

The primary role of the outplacement counselor is stated simply: Prepare the candidate for all the eventualities of a job search. The objective: give the individual a competitive edge in the job market. In reality, the role of outplacement is much more complex. It can encompass such nebulous activities as hand-holding, back-patting and rear-kicking, as well as such tangible activities as campaign-planning, résumé preparation, and interview rehearsal.

Drake Beam Morin, Inc., based in New York and a leader in the field, calls outplacement counseling: "A systematic process by which terminated employees are assisted in successfully finding new employment. It is designed to effect a smooth transition by helping individuals relocate to challenging and rewarding positions within a reasonable period of time and with a minimum of stress."

Costello, Erdlen & Co. Inc., an aggressive Northeastern human resources organization, describes outplacement as "a service which provides terminated employees with the knowledge and professional guidance to approach the job market in a disciplined manner in order to find and obtain a new position in a minimum amount of time."

Of course, some embittered executives might want to include in the definition a reference to "corporate undertakers." But you get the idea.

In a sense, outplacement is defined by the offerings of individual firms. While the variety is extensive, the standard components are fairly well circumscribed. Generally, among the strong points you should be looking for in any firm are:

- Advice on adjusting to the problems and stress of job termination and subsequent job search
- Analysis of your particular skills, achievements, qualifications, experience
- Development of career goals and objectives
- General career and job environment choices

- Execution and control of your personal marketing plan, maintaining proper records
- Insight into the specific job market for your targeted field
- Test-taking preparation and evaluation
- Skills and techniques to succeed in the job interview, creating a strong pitch letter and résumé
- Oral and written communication skills, development and rehearsal of effective oral presentations
- Counsel on deportment and dress, getting through prospective employers' defenses
- The development of contacts and networking
- Identifying appropriate target companies and individuals
- Responding to classified ads, communicating with executive recruiters, personnel consultants
- Negotiation of job offers
- Such support services as typing, reproduction, and mailing services, secretarial, telephone, and message services, office space and a reference library.

All that is well and good, but what exactly do those general activities include. Well, OPC staff consultants will first sit down with you and help you identify previous accomplishments, both personal and professional. They'll help you probe your own ideas on where you are in your career and, more importantly, where you want to be. They'll lead you in formulating a strategy to get where you want to go, cajole you into taking the first steps in that direction, and force you to conduct a disciplined search in accordance with systems that have worked successfully for thousands of clients who've preceded you.

Sometimes those systems are so well formulated they require a manual the size of a small-town telephone directory to explain them. They're just like the systematic approaches you'd use to develop a management project. Assess strengths and weaknesses. Set goals and objectives. Develop a strategy. Prepare the material (in this case letters, résumé, and contact lists). Evaluate options and alternatives. Take action. Follow up. Monitor results.

By now you know, OPC firms won't go out and pound the pavement for you. They will provide valuable aid in several areas, not the least of which psychologists say comes under the heading of "mental health." Outplacement gives you a security blanket of body parts when you need them most—a helping hand, a receptive ear, a shoulder to lean on. It also provides a foot to the rear when you need a shot of adrenaline to get your job search in gear.

The whole concept of outplacement is designed to minimize the trauma of transition for you (and your family) as you prepare to tackle a new direction in your life. It encourages a positive approach to the new situation, and gives you a silver-lining perspective when dark clouds have gathered everywhere. Right from the start, outplacement services soften the blow, help you land on your feet, and keep those peds on the ground.

No matter how tough you picture yourself, discharge from a job is a major life change, akin to divorce and death and other stressful events that try the soul. Outplacement helps to wash away some of the depression, stops the out-of-control feeling and helplessness that is common to these situations, gives a quick dose of "new meaning" to your world turned upside down.

Outplacement firms have honed their psychological skills as more and more devastating experiences get written into the book of termination. Their methods concentrate on warding off that crippling sense of self-pity that's part of an initial firing response. Their approaches attack the feelings of disbelief and anger and despair and aim to replace them with self-confidence and reassurance and hope.

OPENING NEW JOB HORIZONS

Psychologically, outplacement is a balm. Intellectually, it can also expose you to new directions, suggestions, ideas, options, opportunities—maybe some crazy dreams you never even admitted you had. While you were a manager concentrating on your management duties and responsibilities, you may not have had the time or the inclination to follow changing trends, to keep abreast of emerging businesses and industries, to look behind the front-page headlines to the human interest stories in business unfolding in the inside sections. Outplacement nudges you into looking in those nooks and crannies for opportunities that fit you. You'll find (but only with effort on your part) new avenues to explore for personal and professional satisfaction. New channels in which to put your constructive endeavors for a job search. Outplacement encourages you to take an extended trip down the river of your own skills and capabilities and preferences. You explore the deep waters of your own desires, the alternative pathways you could take as you put your job search into motion.

You get other benefits, tangible and intangible, from outplacement. You get the experience and wisdom of others who have been through the trial and know the way to emerge a winner. You get a structure and a system in which to operate, similar to the one you're used to as a manager. You get a game plan with alternatives and options so you don't end up thrown for loss after loss once you've been initially sacked. You even get tips on how to break the news to the home team (spouse, kids, family) so they stay on an even psychological keel as well.

The bottom line of outplacement is this: You get a faster, easier, more routine route out of unemployment and into a new job.

ALL THAT GLITTERS . . .

All this, of course, is the ideal. And nothing in life, Bo Derek notwithstanding, is a pure ideal 10: There are warts in outplacement. One thing to remember is that outplacement firms are, in general, hired by the company that is firing the pink slips at the ranks of managers—at you.

Your company may very well have strong altruistic reasons for helping the objects of a RIF by paying for outplacement services. It may feel a moral compulsion to help. Or a sense of family and loyalty. On the other hand, a company can benefit in several other, more tangible ways. For one, outplacement can help avoid messy and expensive lawsuits. It can improve the morale and productivity of the remaining troops by emphasizing that Captain Bligh isn't at the helm of the corporate ship.

Severance pay can be reduced by finding old employees new jobs quickly, and an objective approach to severance can preclude excessive payouts. Outplacement can also lessen the chances of unpleasantness, tension, and even badmouthing by placing terminated executives in off-site offices away from former colleagues and staff.

Finally, outplacement tempers potential unfavorable publicity, and sends signals to the rest of the business world (customers, vendors, industry competitors) that the organization takes care of its bloodletting in a professional manner.

What matters this to you? Simply that you should know outplacement isn't a one-way street. Don't be shy in taking advantage of every benefit you can derive from it. You're not accepting charity.

WHAT OUTPLACEMENT WON'T DO FOR YOU

Right off the bat, you should realize that an outplacement firm is not going to find you a job. That's not its job. That's yours. If you go into the relationship with unrealistic expectations, you're sure to be disappointed.

Approach this partnership with your eyes wide open. Study the claims (biggest, pioneer, 97 percent of clients get jobs, individualized service, etc.) as if you were watching the Isuzu television commercials where the salesman delivers his spiel and the subheads indicate the verbal comments may not convey the entire truth.

Remember no matter what the expressed philosophy ("We're here to help employees"), nobody is a philanthropist in this business. It's just that, a business. They treat it as such. So should you. You should go in with your eyes open, fully aware of what outplacement counseling organizations *will not* do for you.

For one, they're not personnel recruiting firms or executive placement organizations. (See the definitional differences at the end of this chapter). They don't have a list of job openings that they'll try to match you to (although at least one, Drake Beam, has a job bank which can prove helpful). Their goal is to point you in the direction of appropriate employment, give you career counseling, not turn up a job for the sake of your having a job.

Every outplacement firm has its own systems and programs. But it's more an art than a science. No one can guarantee when, or even if, you'll get a job. Even the common rule of thumb that it takes one month of searching for every $10,000 in salary is proven more in the exception.

Outplacement also doesn't serve as a counseling substitute for such problems as drinking, underperformance, interpersonal disputes, and the like. They are not hired as a quick fix for personal personnel problems.

Ask ten different people about their outplacement experiences, and you're likely to come up with ten different opinions ranging from "lifesaver" to "charlatans." You've seen some of the benefits that the typical OPC offers and how such firms describe themselves. Now listen in as several "candidates" who have been through the experience describe it.

ON THE POSITIVE SIDE

• "Very few people have the discipline to go through the process of finding a job while they're home wearing jeans. Discipline is the key. It's hard to come by, and only gets reinforced by habit, which is what you get with outplacement."

• "The first thing in outplacement counseling is discussion—how you got where you are, why, strengths, weaknesses, the usual. But what you really need is the boosting they give, the hand-holding. At that point you are as low as you can go. The whole process is based on taking baby steps, not jumping in, in one fell swoop. Outplacement makes sure you do it the right way."

• "Years ago, people thought only deadbeats and the lame ended up in outplacement. All that has changed today."

ON THE NEGATIVE SIDE

• "They seem to emphasize that to get a new job, you can't be yourself. You must put on an act, wear a new suit, a power tie, make no waves, kowtow to potential employers."

• "It [outplacement] was an eye-opening experience. The bottom line was that I'd have to carefully package myself, like laundry soap in the supermarket, to attract a buyer for my NEW, IMPROVED talents. I was told the one who gets the job is often the one who does a better job of selling an image."

• "You have to find your own job. No one else is going to do it for you. Outplacement shifts the problem from the mother organization to you. They are a salve for the corporate conscience."

MAXIMIZING THE OUTPLACEMENT EXPERIENCE

Now that you know some of the pros and cons of the OPC field, you'll be better able to take advantage of what its members have to offer. Here are some additional suggestions to keep in mind as you prepare for the experience.

Recognize that outplacement firms run the gamut from confessional types that are geared mainly to dry terminated tears to product-package types which gussy up the ex-execs image so they get chosen for new teams.

While the group support you get from the outplacement exercise is valuable, be prepared for a lot of gallows humor and in some cases insensitivity. Your experience may be akin to the individual who labeled his group "like a college fraternity."

On the other hand, stories have made the rounds about the competitiveness involved in outplacement—about stolen letters, misplaced messages, leads that fall into hands for which they were not intended. Treat the information you develop with the importance it deserves. It could mean your livelihood.

An outplacement firm's livelihood is predicated on serving its main client—the corporation that pays its fees. So be careful about badmouthing your former employer or screwing up in any way that might reflect poorly on your previous company. Outplacement personnel have-been known to react negatively to such negativism.

You'll get along fine as long as you follow the system, take advantage of the tools they offer, and never expect more from outplacement than it is geared to give.

But do take advantage of what they offer, especially when they include a physical setting, such as an office to go to and use, or a conference room to discuss matters with your peers. One of the strongest negative psychological reactions to displacement is confusion and loss of direction. You can combat these destructive demons by having a place to go every day for which you dress up like the manager you've always been. You leave the house as you did before you lost your job. You carry your briefcase and work with papers like before. You go to a business address and drink coffee and talk with colleagues, just as you did at your former company. Behaving normally helps calm the real feelings of turmoil that surround a job loss.

One additional fact of outplacement firms often goes untapped, and is in fact controversial within the industry. Some OPCs have ties to executive recruiting firms. The defenders of such a relationship claim that the two complement each other. Outplacement taps recruitment when possible matches exist. Recruitment feeds off outplacement when spots are available.

The critics point to the potential conflict of interest, with outplacement firms pushing their clients in only one direction and recruitment organizations pulling in fees for the same. Some companies that offer both recruitment and outplacement services solve the problem by not accepting fees from both ends for the same placement.

The controversy or conflict, though, isn't your problem. You want the quickest way to get back on track in your career. So ask about any other personnel ties, written or unwritten, from your outplacement firm.

SPECIAL OUTPLACEMENT PROGRAMS

While you're at it, ask for a menu of programs from the organization you become a client of. As with any business, outplacement firms always seek to set themselves apart from the competition. One way is by developing unique programs (or at least fancy labels). Make sure you review the entire selection of offerings at the firm you use. Don't be afraid to ask if they don't have something you've heard or read about. Here are some examples.

Psychological evaluations and testing services are becoming more prevalent these days, but are not universally accepted or offered. Especially if you're considering a career or industry change, this is an area to explore.

Spouse counseling is sometimes offered. One wife of a terminated executive said she had been more inclined to anger than her husband. A valuable program in many cases is a group where the "significant other" can vent his or her feelings.

Psychological coping counseling of your own usually with professionals in the field, sometimes utilizing an academic or specialty organization.

Extra help as when a candidate is "double-teamed" during preparation to give him or her the benefit of three heads rather than two. Or follow-up coaching that extends beyond the time limits of group programs.

Proprietary databases where some companies are so specialized they keep track of a particular industry or geographic region by developing information that only they (and their clients—that's you) have access to.

Some companies even trademark and copyright their own names for programs or outplacement tools, such as:

- Job Search By Objectives (Cambridge Human Resource Group, Inc., Northbrook, IL)

- The Career Challenge (The Career Development Team, Inc., New York City)
- Management Outplacement Resources Extended (MORE) (Comwell Co., Florham Park, NJ)
- One company, New Directions, Inc., of Boston, even works closely with Outward Bound, a national leadership/self-help organization specializing in combining business with back to nature.

Beampines, Inc., in New York tries to pinpoint the "closet entrepreneur" with a series of psychological tests. Beampines will give advice to those who pass the muster, direct them to lawyers, accountants, and venture capital firms, and in some instances even invest a bob or two themselves in a new venture.

Seagate Associates in New Jersey calls its offices an "incubator" for the entrepreneurial. They offer consulting support, market research, competitive analysis, customer identification, franchise advice, and even direction to government-associated small-business investment firms.

If you prefer power breakfasts on your schedule, J.J. Gallagher Associates in New York sets up meetings with speakers to expose clients and staff to suggestions and advice from an array of job-hunt experts.

The point is that, like snowflakes, no two outplacement firms are exactly the same and no two programs will have the same impact on you. If you have a choice, do your homework, and choose wisely.

SIZING UP AN OPC

The first thing to do is ask around. Seek out opinions from people you know who have been involved with that firm either directly or peripherally. Especially if any friends or former colleagues have utilized the same service, get a reading from them on the pros and cons of that particular firm.

Also ask for references when you can. See what kind of client list the OPC boasts, both companies served and individuals helped.

Now turn your focus from people outside the company to internal personnel. Look at the principals, how long they've been in the business, what kind of credentials they possess. Also ask about the staff. Who will perform the actual counseling? What are their specialties? Do they also have corporate experience, which is a major plus? What are the numbers involved in terms of staff handling, i.e., will it be a one-on-one situation or group involvement.

The company itself must also come under scrutiny. What other services does it offer besides outplacement, and what percentage of the total revenues are derived from each service? Is outplacement its number-one priority? What's the style of the organization, button down or flexible (remember you need "chemistry" for the relationship to work)? Do you feel a "comfort level" when you deal with the organization?

Does the company specialize in a particular industry or function or region of the country? This could be a double-edged sword. In certain cases specialization offers concentrated effort. On the other hand it could limit the extent of its aid to you.

What about the programs offered? In terms of group versus individual, there are again two sides to the coin. Groups per se are not bad. The sharing and the interaction can provide needed balance. But always try to get some form of individual attention.

The better the firm, the more special programs it will offer outside the realm of the traditional. But don't overlook asking about the so-called standard services that all top-notch firms should offer: office space, secretarial, phones, copy machine, mailing capacity, library with reference books, psychological counseling.

(*Note:* Some firms offer office space, but set a time limit on how often and how long you can use it. That could definitely cramp your search, so it's an important consideration.)

Finally, don't be afraid to ask for a track record. But swallow any statistics with a grain of salt. No company can guarantee you'll get a job through its efforts. If one does, be even more leery. An honest batting average can at least give you an inkling of whether a particular firm is really playing in the major leagues.

FINDING WHAT YOU NEED

In most cases you don't have a choice. The company hires an outplacement firm. You use it. Simple. But there are a lot of fish in the outplacement sea.

If you want to see the difference between the whales and the minnows, check out the Directory of Outplacement Firms, compiled and published by Kennedy & Kennedy, Inc., publishers of *Consultant News* and *Executive Recruiter News.* This pink-sheathed reference (pink slip, get it?) can be had by writing James Kennedy at Templeton Road, Fitzwilliam, NH 03447.

One noteworthy part for a recently terminated manager appears in Section II. That's where the firms are listed which accept individual clients as opposed to corporate. With the former you pay the freight, not your company. The same publisher also produces *Directory of Executive Recruiters* and a catalog of Executive Search Books. All can be homework helpers.

As you wander through that maze of potential search sources, you should also know how several other job-hunting organizations are defined:

- Employment agencies—also called placement and personnel service or consulting firms. Oriented to finding jobs. Builds lists of candidates with advertisements or referrals. Placement fee sometimes paid by candidate. Fee contingent on accepted offer.
- Contingency search—a/k/a personnel recruitment, placement, consulting. Fee paid by employer on acceptance of offer. Employer oriented, but assists selected individuals.
- Retained or executive search—works for employer, gets fee even if candidate isn't hired, sometimes gets expenses.
- Temporary service—provides staffing assistance on assignments. Client usually billed at hourly rate.
- Career consulting—usually individuals pay the fee for services ranging from career strategy development to résumé preparation.
- Job listing—firms that clip classified ads from publications and sell lists to individuals seeking positions.

THE LANGUAGE OF OUTPLACEMENT

Besides definitions of the major players in the job search game, you should also understand the vernacular of the trade. Knowing the jargon and initials that pop up will add another measure of certainty and familiarity to an otherwise disorienting experience.

The following lists are not to be memorized for a pop quiz, but they will prove helpful in your overall search for a return to normalcy—and employment. If personnel types start throwing initials at you, here are the ones to know (you can look up the organizations in *Gale's Directory,* which most public libraries have in their reference section:)

AACD	American Association of Counseling & Development
ABVE	American Board of Vocational Experts
AMC	Association of Management Consultants
AOCF	Association of Outplacement Consulting Firms
APGA	American Personnel & Guidance Association
ASTD	American Society for Training & Development
EMA	Employment Management Association
IMC	Institute of Management Consultants
NACPR	National Association of Corporate & Professional Recruits
NECA	National Employment Counselors Association
SERC	Society of Executive Recruiting Consultants
SPMC	Society of Professional Management Consultants

To the definitions and initials, you can add outplacement buzzwords which will ease your search experience. Here are some key ones:

Assessment. System using written or verbal format for evaluating professional experience, individual preferences, potential goals.

Back-office support. Such services as secretary, library, word processing, typing, copying, telephone.

Blitz. When an outplacement firm piles on the fuel to propel a candidate more quickly through a job-hunt campaign.

Bridge money. Similar to term used in real estate transactions. You get a special loan at a special rate for expenses incurred due to termination, like moving.

Broadcast material. Usually covers letters and résumés sent to a large number of prospective employers.

Candidate/Client. That's you.

Chemistry. You might hear this as the reason for termination. Could be a personality, character, or style mismatch. Also could be an excuse.

Continuation of benefits. One thing you should be looking for from your former employer. Get as many provisions for extending benefits (such as medical and dental insurance, stock options, savings program) as you can. Then see if there are methods to convert to individual payment. (See Chapter 5)

Counselor/Consultant. That's them.

Dehiring. What outplacement counseling was called in its former life.

Demassing. Term used to describe large-scale dismissals, sometimes involving entire departments or functions.

Downsizing. Common term to describe company reducing its size because of economic cutbacks, product termination, trend to "lean and mean," and so forth.

Drifting. You become a drifter when you take an unusually long time to find new employment opportunities. Most outplacement firms call a blitz formation for a drifter.

Employment-at-will. As you saw in Chapter 6, the idea that the employer can hire and fire without reasons. Becoming a dinosaur doctrine.

Exit statement. A written statement agreed to by company and individual stating reasons individual left company. Usually includes the questions you should have been asked while still on the job.

Feeder. The individual who coordinates the relationship between the outplacement firm and the terminating company.

Group outplacement. Service usually provided to lower-level corporate types, but you may be involved if your firm had a large reduction in staff. Ranges anywhere from a half-day seminar to a three- or even five-day workshop. Groups small, particularly for managerial level. Often accompanied or followed by individual consultations. Ask for the latter.

Head hunter. Slang for executive search firm recruitment specialist.

In-house outplacement. Program for individual or group outplacement services by your own company. Usually includes HRD people or staff members who are trained to provide outplacement services.

Mail campaign. Starts when you send out résumés and cover letters to contacts, executive recruiters, advertisements and your network.

Market strategy. Your plan for launching yourself into the marketplace to find employers most likely to hire you.

Networking. The single most important part of your job search. Contacting as many people as possible to obtain referrals to companies, job leads, and other information pertinent to your hunt.

Reduction in force. Cutback involving group or groups of employees. Terminations for business or economic reasons to reduce operating budgets.

Referral agents. Professional resource people who handle situations not under the aegis of outplacement counselors (such as alcohol, marriage, financial problems).

Retail outplacement. This is when you pay for the service yourself. Generally offers programs similar to corporate outplacement services, except you foot the bill.

Salary continuation. Regular salary paid after termination for a specified time to allow the individual to find a new job. Severance is similar, but may come in lump sum. You need your tax man or woman if you have a choice.

Shoppers/Tire-kickers. An increasingly common phenomenon. Practice on the part of sponsoring clients to use more than one firm for outplacement services. Very often results in a departing employee (you) being given a list of two or three or more outplacement firms to visit. Then you make the decision about which one is best.

CHAPTER 11

Minding Your
Own Business

Entrepreneurship—
Possible Feast or
Potential Famine

GOTTA get back to mind the store."

How many times have you, as a corporate manager, spoken that familiar phrase? While it doesn't accurately fit your job, you've almost certainly tossed out this colorful figure of speech. It's a common sign-off after a business luncheon. You may have used it to wind up a meeting with clients or customers. Or you may even have said it when you were just visiting one of your peers down the hall.

Is it just a sign-off? Or does saying "mind the store" reveal a secret yearning among nearly all managers for the independence and autonomy that they perceive is the happy lot of business owners?

You've already seen the dichotomy. In Chapters 8 and 9 you read about the plethora of options and opportunities that are open to you. Yet in Chapter 10 you saw that outplacement consultants interviewed for this book asserted that displaced managers usually seem to be bound by hoops of steel to their occupations and industries. They often ache to become enveloped again in the warm cocoon of companies of the same size and same type as those that fired them.

An early task for outplacement counselors is to remove these blinders or correct this tunnel vision. They want clients to be more flexible about the kinds of jobs they're willing to seek out and accept. That mission is not just to make their outplacing easier. They've often found through evaluations and testing that certain managers have held positions for many years that make far less than full use of their talents—jobs that have tried to fit square pegs into octagonal holes.

Some displaced middle managers, especially those over age fifty, feel immediate relief when they're whizzed out the end of the corporate laundry chute. Their sudden discharges revive long-buried free spirits and cravings for independence. They begin to dream a different American dream. That's not the dream of duplicating the rags-to-riches rise of Horatio Alger. Rather, it's that elusive other dream—being one's own boss.

This chapter examines self-employment options, not just for the discharged or over-fifty, but for all managers—even the ones who have remained on the job. It gives you the informational wherewithal to help you judge whether or not a business of your own might be the right choice for you. It will help you, among other things, to compare owning a business to being a manager in the world of far-flung corporations.

You'll read about three major possibilities: starting your own business, buying an existing company, and investing in the franchise game. Each of these options has its own promises and pitfalls. None of them may fit you like the proverbial glove. But you'll be able to make more-educated decisions after you've absorbed the information here, tested your own mental attitudes against certain psychic qualities needed for successful independent ownership, and self-assessed your own entrepreneurial traits.

ARE YOU THE RIGHT TYPE?

Entrepreneurs, those individuals who start up businesses independently or operate as ultimate decision-makers in businesses they buy, have been studied, probed, and prodded by psychologists, motivational specialists, personality diagnosticians, and even psychoanalysts. These professionals have found very few traits that appear to be absolutely dependable as identifiers of successful entrepreneurs. Yet, when the analytical dust has settled, certain recurring characteristics do emerge.

Unfortunately, though, just being the right type to run a business of your own does not insure that you'll be successful should you take the plunge. There's much more to running a business than traits, qualities, and characteristics. If you do possess the same ones as most successful entrepreneurs, then that fact should give you an added measure of confidence. You'll see that the entrepreneurial traits in you set you apart from those who only achieve success and happiness when they're wrapped in what they perceive (often incorrectly) as a corporate security blanket.

To give yourself a reading on your own qualities for entrepreneurship, check off each item in the following list with which you can identify. Give yourself a comfort-level rating from 1 to 5—1 being a very inexact reflection of yourself in the question, and 5 being almost a mirror image.

Then, get some others to rate you, too, before you jump to any conclusions that you're the perfect type and dash out to invest in a franchise or a for-sale company, or to start up your own business. Be sure to include among the raters your spouse (if you're married), a golf or tennis partner, and a colleague with whom you've worked cheek by jowl for several years. Their opinions are immensely valuable—in truth, critical. They may see you in entirely different lights from the way that you envision yourself.

Qualities-of-Business-Owners Rating Scale
- Am I a self-starter? (Do you do things your own way without needing to have someone tell you to get on the ball and get going?)

- Am I a good organizer? (Can you plan and get things lined up on your own or do you need both big and little plans laid out for you?)
- Am I a leader? (Have you consistently volunteered for tasks, or do you just carry out jobs that come your way?)
- Am I a hard worker? (Do you put in as many hours as required, whenever required, to get jobs done or would you prefer to be a nine-to-fiver?)
- Am I a decision-maker? (Have you been able to say yes or no when an important question is on the line, or do you procrastinate in hopes that the problem will fade away?)
- Am I a people-person? (Can you get along with most anybody, or are you constantly turned off by others and essentially work best alone?)
- Am I a stick-to-it type? (Do you finish what you start without being needled by others to complete the project?)

There's no good score or bad score for the qualities listed on this rating scale. Don't bother adding up your 5's, 4's, or 1's. The scale is not a quiz. It's designed purposely to get you to think seriously about yourself and your suitability for entrepreneurship. It helps you answer the critically important question "Am I the right type?" Every checkpoint underscores an important requirement for success in business ownership.

In fact, you may be discerning enough to see that many questions also apply to traits that top-notch managers of corporations should also possess. You can get along in the corporate world with a smattering of zeros on the rating scale. You'll need higher marks on every single one to make the grade as a business owner.

Another primary difference, too, is that in the corporate environment you can get away from it all for a week, or even several weeks (some big-city bankers take off for six) without the company's sales or income accounts registering a blip. As a proprietor, until you've reached a critical mass, absence is likely to send both revenues and profits off the chart—on the side toward oblivion. Despite commonly held pictures of business owners, an hour or two of daydreaming now and then may be as much as you'll ever get a chance to enjoy. Unlike managing in a big corporation, you can't even turn your mind off at night.

HALLMARKS OF ENTREPRENEURS

Those traits necessary for entrepreneurial success may not be exclusively held hallmarks of the business owner. However, some traits, according to the experts, do seem to separate the individuals who make a go of "business-for-self" from company-oriented middle managers.

Few people leap immediately into proprietorship, other than way back when they had their summertime Kool Aid stands. Almost all entrepreneurs serve apprenticeships by working in company-type, organized environments. Something, though, triggers entrepreneurs to jump ship and start off on their own. Frequently, it's getting fired that is the proximate cause. You should not, though, interpret your getting severed from your company as giving you similar common ground. Most likely, your getting fired came about, as you know, through no fault of your own.

For entrepreneurs, getting axed in a restructuring is not the root cause of most dismissals or resignations, according to the recorders of such data. They usually were shoved out of the corporate workplace for political reasons: they just couldn't get along well enough with their bosses. Or, in other instances, their bosses shut their ears to new ideas.

Out of pure frustration, entrepreneurial types often decide to skip out of company confinement so that they can put their "big ideas" into action. One example: the dean of an undergraduate school of business could not persuade the university trustees to finance nonresident extension courses. Convinced of the validity of his "big idea," the dean founded a correspondence school which blossomed and grew for many years.

Another situation: a once-in-a-lifetime opportunity unexpectedly surfaces. An offer of substantial financial backing with no strings attached (at least until the venture meets certain goals) springs corporate managers loose. That one-time offer enables them to bring into being and take to market their favorite widgets, the prototypes of which they assembled in the privacy of their garages.

SIMILARITIES AND DIFFERENCES— OWNERS VERSUS MANAGERS

You should be cautious about identifying with any of these trigger points when evaluating your prospects as a new business owner, whether still employed or pounding the pavement. It's easy to make a case that there are more similarities between corporate managers and entrepreneurs than there are differences. If you proceed on that assumption, you'll make a grave mistake. Certainly it's true, as the saying goes, that entrepreneurs pull their pants on one leg at a time, just as you do. But that's not a relevant consideration.

The differences between entrepreneurs and corporate managers which really count are identifiable and critical. They fall under a number of headings such as:

An insatiable desire for autonomy. Many entrepreneurs when employed by corporations are continually in trouble with authority. They have difficult times stay-

ing within the rules of organizations. That specific characteristic often catapults them out of confining companies and into the freedom of being their own bosses. Needs
for autonomy is a trait that may also bear the seeds of
their ultimate demise when the business succeeds. Steve
Jobs, founder of Apple Computer, hired from Pepsi-Cola
the man whose organizing and marketing skills were essential to save Apple from collapse. The clash between
them about corporate cultures ended with Jobs leaving
Apple, his big idea.

A high tolerance, even a yen, for risk taking. That
trait should get you to nod your head because, according
to Dun & Bradstreet's statistics, a mere 44% of new
businesses survive more than five years. Offsetting the
rational interpretation that independent business owners are gamblers is some evidence that they're highly
confident, as well as driven, in their abilities and in their
products. An Ohio State University professor says that
entrepreneurs don't see risks; they see opportunities that
they believe they can control.

*An instinct for making the right choices among alter-
natives.* Unlike corporate managers, who prefer the
structure of preset corporate goals and annual, or even
longer-term, plans to reach them, entrepreneurs are
usually comfortable bending with the wind, moving
toward ill-defined goals without really understanding how
they're going to get to them.

An extra measure of persuasiveness. If anyone needs
charm and grace, it's the entrepreneur. Reason? Few individuals can get started in business without access to
OPM—other people's money. That particular trait does
not seem to square with the stereotype of entrepreneurs
as white-coated inventors hunched over their lab tables—
loners. Those caricature entrepreneurs, if they exist at
all, are the ones more likely to fail. The winners are
evangelical types. Back in the nineteenth century, they
would be the ones who set up their tents on the out-

skirts of town while their assistants sold snake oil as the price of admission. Then they preached that old-time religion.

In addition to checking yourself against the qualities and traits you'll need to be successful should you go into business for yourself, you should also compare the advantages and disadvantages of that strategy with those of managing in a sizable corporation.

An earlier section in this chapter commented upon the total time consumption that a business of your own takes compared to managing in a large corporation. For those of you who have put in sixty- to eighty-hour weeks, traveled all over the world on business, put up with irascible bosses, been moved from one location to another a half-dozen times for the greater glory of the corporation, that comparison may ring as hollow for you as the clanging sound of an empty 100-gallon oil drum bouncing down the highway.

However, it is a true one. Even the twelve-hour corporate day shrinks when contrasted with the time you'll expend as a business owner. Let no one kid you—owning your own business takes total commitment.

There are, though, many advantages. You would not only derive a feeling of independence from business ownership, but you'd also feel a much greater sense of accomplishment as you see your business develop. You would be, of course, your own boss and couldn't be fired, even though you'll experience days when you wish you could. Few things pump in more personal pleasure than the pride of ownership. You've felt it when you've driven home a new car with the admiring eyes of your neighbors upon you. You've felt pride in owning your house or apartment. That tremendous satisfaction from business ownership would expand even more as you saw the products and services you offered being accepted and valued in the marketplace.

Another advantage of being in business for yourself

is flexibility. You can adapt to a change, adopt a new idea, or acquire a new process or product quickly. You don't need to turn to your boss, or some unwieldy executive committee or stubborn board for permission each time you want to try something new. You can drop a failing product or plan just as quickly. You're not focused by momentum or longtime customers into keeping losing lines going, as is frequently the case in large companies. It's easier to get the QE 2 to make a U-turn in the Hudson River than it is to get some of those dinosaur-size companies to change course.

Not to be overlooked among the advantages: you can pay yourself a salary—and keep the profits, too.

EVER HAD TO MEET A PAYROLL?

But to borrow a phrase from the best tradition of the legal profession—"on the other hand"—business ownership does have some distinct disadvantages compared to corporate management. When was the last time, as a company manager, that you had to meet a payroll? That fearsome task in a big-company environment is the responsibility of a legal entity—the corporation.

In your own business, you must meet the payroll week after week. You may be able to get an outside accountant or service to take off your hands the burden of calculating withholding, FICA, and unemployment taxes, among other details. But it's your responsibility to get the money to the bank, to your workers, to the IRS, and to get it there on time.

You'll have creditors—vendors, mortgage holders, landlords, and ever-present tax collectors. They all have to be satisfied. In the corporate environment those worries are spread around. The responsibility in case of oversight or failure ultimately rests in the hands of the officers and directors. In your own business, as the saying goes, "the buck stops here"—right at your door, right on your desk, right in your checkbook.

You'll now be the final decision maker. You can't share the role with others as you can in a corporation. You can't delegate authority to make decisions until you have individuals to whom you can delegate. In short, no CYA decisions. The responsibility for the results of your decisions remains with you. You'll be all alone to bear the losses of poor judgment, or setbacks due to adverse economic conditions over which you have no control. You'll have to determine how to battle competitors and accept the consequences—whatever they are.

Even should you buy an ongoing business staffed with experienced people who have been carrying out the routine grunt-work for years, you can't escape responsibility. You may acquire a pile of headaches with that going concern. (Some of these pitfalls will be covered later in this chapter.)

THE NAME OF THE "OWN BUSINESS" GAME IS MONEY

According to the credit rating firm Dun & Bradstreet, 90 percent of all business failures are due to poor management. The second biggest cause of companies being forced into the deep six is lack of capital. When you think of it, though, the second cause is clearly linked to the first. It's poor management to start a new business without adequate capital.

Don't delude yourself that the world of big-bucks investors will beat a path to your door when you decide to open shop. It won't. The sure fact is that the most critical start-up source of seed capital will be your own personal resources—credit and cash.

During an interview for this book, one budding entrepreneur said, "If I get fired and come out of the company with $200,000 in cash, I can leverage that to 2 million." Yes, he can, with a hatful of ifs. If he's got the temperament (and the right stuff) to watch his $200,000 dwindle to nearly nothing under the pressure of initial expenses. If he's very lucky, or if he has easy access to capital sources, then he may be able to leverage himself without losing working control of the new venture.

What has happened today is that many separation packages pour out substantial caches of cash to discharged individuals who have put in a couple of decades or so at the same old stand. Those bundles of greenbacks, of course, represent lump-sum payments, 401(k) plan distributions, cash value of stock purchases or stock options and other goodies.

When individuals who have been accustomed to living on above-the-median incomes suddenly get a chunk of cash, they are likely to hear the siren call of their subliminal dreams and fantasies for independence. Many take the plunge into entrepreneurship. Most such well-endowed people, outplacement consultants say, are more likely to seek going concerns or franchises to buy than to start from scratch. That's especially true of discharged middle managers who have reached their mid-fifties.

One such person interviewed had been a manager in GE's News Bureau which, as was related in Chapter 7, was completely erased in a restructuring. "My separation package," he said, "included half-pay until I became eligible for the retirement plan. It also continued health and medical coverage for a year. I began to think about starting my own PR firm with a couple of others who'd been let go. But as I looked at it, calculated the costs of starting up, thought about the sixty-to-eighty-hour weeks and the effects on my family, I realized that by the time

I really got going in my own business, it would be time to retire." This particular manager decided that a start-up business of his own was not the route he would take.

YOUR MONEY PLAN FOR LIVING EXPENSES

Make no mistake about it: despite all the hullabaloo about banks bursting with money which they'd now like to lend to U.S. borrowers, and about venture capitalists lurking in the bushes eager to shower cash on entrepreneurs with big ideas or new widgets, the sound is different from the reality. Your management expertise, your idea for a business, and/or your desire to bring it all into a functioning concern, are plainly not enough. At least one all-important measure of your real worth, in the eyes of all moneylenders, is just as important—your willingness to invest your own cash.

The entrepreneurs' own cash investment underlies most success stories of managers who left organizational stability to strike out on their own. Another important factor: they did so by laying the groundwork for the new enterprise long before they cut loose from the regular paycheck. Some entrepreneurs planned for years before taking the road to independence and self-employment. So, if you're among those who have been kicked out into the street, and are contemplating business ownership for your next career, you're already late getting under way. You've had a couple of high hard ones whistled through the strike zone while your bat has been resting on your shoulder. You must get your priorities right to keep yourself from whiffing at the third fast ball. And one of those priorities is a plan to manage your personal living resources.

At least a dozen books are published each year on how to start your own business. Most of them are written by individuals who have gone into businesses for themselves and succeeded. Many are autobiographical. Because books about failures don't sell, you will only see books which report nothing but success.

When it comes to the story behind the story, though, highlights are plentiful and details are sparse. When the book turns to how the authors raised the money to bootstrap themselves out of their routine jobs to make millions as entrepreneurs, the facts are even less evident. There'll be a chapter or two about the importance of capital. You may even find a list of names and addresses of venture capital firms. Authors, though, remain strangely silent about exactly where the money came from for their starts.

Journalistically that makes sense. Who wants to read stories about meteoric rises in self-employment should the authors let on that they were already wealthy? "Riches to riches" doesn't sell. "Rags to riches" does. Would-be entrepreneurs don't find the innermost secrets of successful entrepreneurship in such books. That innermost secret is money—or ready access to it.

You must realize, too, before you buy out your local bookstore's supply of "success books," that the authors were not suddenly caught in the buzzsaw of corporate downsizing. Normally they took time to plan, organize, gather financial resources, and establish credit before they jumped into the entrepreneurial pool.

Say, however, that you've determined that you're the right "own business" type. Add to that the happy circumstance of a fine severance package including a six-figure lump-sum payment. Say, further, that you've plenty of equity in your home and funds set aside for your children's education—or they've completed college. Then what? Do you still have to go through the mind-numbing task of working out your living-money plan? You bet you do!

Seldom do new businesses support themselves right from the start, much less their owners' living expenses.

Nor do going concerns when purchased usually generate sufficient margins to pay their buyers well from the day they man the helm. That's a matter of economics. The owners who sell out highly profitable businesses can claim premium prices. Profitable businesses attract competitors to bid against you to acquire them. Leveraging your own capital contribution and probably the firm's assets after acquisition, means you'll need to generate larger than customary cash flows to service and repay the debt. As one banker says, "It's easy to borrow money. But it's hell to pay it back."

Taking the third option, buying a franchise, may not be as risky as starting your own company or buying a going concern. However, even the blue-chip franchises aren't risk-free. Moreover, a franchise may be far less glamorous and afford less independence than you crave.

The plain fact is that the only way to get started in any of the three routes to business ownership with a margin of safety is to be sure that your personal living expenses are covered *first*. One long-held opinion has it that money you shell out going into business for yourself should be money you can afford to lose.

So, get out a long columnar sheet, like those legal-size, greenish-gray pads you see accountants scratching their pencils on, and get started. Set up your headings, a column for each, as follows: monthly sources of income, monthly expenses, readily available liquid assets.

Then begin to list under the income heading the cash which you can count on receiving each month.

Checklist of Income Sources

Separation pay _____   Spouse's salary _____

Dividends _____   Interest income _____

Retirement pay _____   Rental income _____

Social Security _____   Unemployment _____

Miscellaneous _____

Now use the following memory jogger to list your monthly expenses.

Checklist of Monthly Expenses

Groceries _____	Consumer loans _____
Mortgage/rent _____	Life insurance _____
Heat/light/power _____	Medical insurance _____
Clothing _____	Transportation _____
Property taxes _____	Contributions _____
Home insurance _____	Fees and dues _____
Auto loans _____	Other _____
Auto insurance _____	Estimated income tax ___

These items are not all-inclusive. Review your canceled checks for the past year and add missing expenses to your list. As you review, begin to mark those expenses which are virtually inescapable. Checkmark those which you can postpone, modify, or just plain eliminate.

Compare your list of income with your list of expenses. Multiply each one by 12 to get your annual amounts. The difference in the totals for a year will have to be covered by your assets. In the "readily available liquid assets" column list them all—bank accounts, equity in your home (only the percent you can borrow), cash value of insurance and other assets. Bear in mind that should you liquidate any of them, you'll reduce your monthly income. Should you borrow on your insurance or the equity in your home, you'll increase your monthly expenses. To the extent that your liquid assets (or those you can borrow against) cover any deficit between your income and expenses for a year with some excess, you have capital which you can use to start up or buy into a business, or invest in a franchise.

Why a year? Every study made shows that new businesses yield zero returns to the owner for at least that period of time. Anyone who thinks that business ownership yields immediate income, and decides to enter the entrepreneurial marathon with that belief, is advised to become very friendly with a bankruptcy lawyer before the twelve months have expired.

A pessimistic outlook? Absolutely. Thirty percent of all new businesses fail in the first year. Only 44 percent make it through five years. And the majority of those which do make it were planned long before the owners quit the safety nets strung under them by regular company paychecks.

CHOOSING THE RIGHT BUSINESS MATCH

So, you've decided you're the right type. You've calculated that you can cover your living expenses for a year without any yield from your new venture. You're ready to dive into the booming world of business ownership. And you have some extra cash or capital assets you can leverage. What type of company should you go into? Should you start up, buy into, or invest in a franchise? Just as important a decision—what kind of product or service can you sell?

Keep in mind an ancient, but apt axiom: people who succeed do so NOT by doing things right, but by choosing the right things to do. For instance, you may be able to design the best computer system for wholesalers to forecast what each of their dealers will buy. But if wholesalers don't want such forecasts, you haven't chosen the right thing to do.

Many prospective entrepreneurs fall into the trap of picking products or services that *they'd like* to manufacture or offer. They don't investigate the marketplace. They don't ask whether anyone has an interest in or can be persuaded to buy what they want to sell. That's why it's crucial to choose the right business to get into before you enter what could turn into a wild goose chase.

Again self-evaluation rears its important head. After examining yourself to determine if you're made of the right stuff to succeed in business for yourself, you must take another step. What special knowledge, skills, aptitudes, and experiences can you bring to bear?

Drag out your résumé. If you've constructed a good one, you've emphasized your accomplishments in it. The critical ones are those that you can use in your business. For example, if one of your accomplishments was "uncovered fraudulent transactions resulting in a $200,000 recovery," you can dismiss that one out of hand. You don't have a business yet to enable you to put that accomplishment to use.

On the other hand, if your résumé shows that you hired five sales reps whose volume grew each year they were under your management, you have a concrete asset of great value to you when you own your own business. You've demonstrated the ability to hire successful sales reps; you've shown you can train and motivate— two excellent skills for any new business owner to have.

Review your professional education and experience, and your hobbies. (Remember Chapter 8.) How does all of your background match with the *current* most favorable opportunities for new businesses? During the early 1980s it was easy to see that the best opportunities were in personal services, electronics, and computers. Suppose you were a human resources or benefits manager employed in a declining rust-belt industry. Your skills in that company or industry are certainly transferable to another. There's been enormous growth in employment-related services. Should you consider starting an employment advisory services company, an outplacement firm, an executive search firm? Should you seek out such a firm to buy? Or should you invest in a franchise for an employment agency?

These are the kinds of self-examinations which you must make to help you find the right match, and make the right choice. Unless you studiously seek and find that match, you're guaranteeing that you'll become another failure statistic.

If you can't readily find the proper match, and you still have the choice, then don't leave the corporate world, no matter how badly it may have treated you lately. If you insist on going out on your own, but can't find the match (or as a displaced middle manager you don't have the time to find it) then take a job at a company that does provide a needed product or service. Pick one in which you have some interest, even if the match may not seem quite right.

At possibly a much lower salary than you thought you could ever live on, you'll get invaluable training and learning experiences before you begin a similar type business on your own. That's a cost of prospective independent ownership that you'll have to absorb. Even at low pay, your risk is far less than if you go off half-cocked into a venture with less than a fifty-fifty chance for survival.

Working for experience in someone else's company doesn't mean you're just marking time. You're getting vital lessons, buying time for *planning,* and reducing your risks. Working in a business for experience is equally good advice when you're considering buying a going concern. Get to know the business first before you leap into the pool. You may be so pleased with the products or services offered that you may end up buying that particular company.

During this essential pause for self- and market-opportunity evaluation, give serious thought to another proposition too: whom do you need to help you get started? Despite all the publicity about the nasty relationships and separations that result from partnerships, it is clearly true that most successful new ventures combine the talents of two or more people (where would Hewlett be without Packard?). Just as the Miami Dolphins during the 1970s had Larry Csonka as Mr. Inside and Mercury Morris as Mr. Outside, so can a teammate or two who have complementary strengths more than double your chances for success.

Evaluate your weaknesses as well as your strengths. Then see if you can plug up your weaknesses with someone else's strong suits. In almost any setting, two heads are better than one. In business, normally, two heads are much, much better than one.

THE MYSTERIOUS MATTER OF BUYING A BUSINESS

Can you achieve the dream of being your own boss by buying a business which is already an ongoing concern? Will taking that route to entrepreneurship let you avoid the headaches, heartaches, and some of the risks of starting from scratch? The twin answers to these twin questions are yes and no.

It has been estimated that some 300,000 companies are put up for sale by their owners each year. Your mission, should you choose to accept it, is to find one that's right for you. How can you get started in that search?

One way to get going is through the business broker route. The numbers just cited of companies for sale have created a burgeoning business of their own—business brokers. In some respects business brokers are similar to real estate brokers. Their primary function is bringing buyers and sellers together. Their secondary function is to smooth out the details of the buy-sell transaction by acting as a go-between for the two parties.

Unlike real estate brokers, though, some business brokers ask for money up front, to be credited against any commission they may later earn. That's double jeopardy for you. If the broker fails to find a satisfactory business for you, you've lost the up-front fees.

As usually occurs when a new industry or occupational specialty springs up, associations of the participants follow not far behind. Business brokers have theirs, too, ranging coast to coast from the International Institute of Business Brokers in Massachusetts to the Institute of Certified Business Brokers in California.

The associations can provide you with some information about their industry. Take it, though, with a grain of salt. Do independent research about any business brokers you contact. Be sure to speak to buyers and sellers they've brought together.

As is true with homes for sale, there are a variety of reasons why businesses come on the market. Those reasons can vary from settling estates of deceased owners to entrepreneurs who want to cash in their chips while they're still ahead of the game.

But don't carry the similarities between these two kinds of brokers too far. The risks of buying a business far exceed the normal ones connected with buying a home. Furthermore, business brokering has drawn considerable, and in some cases well-deserved, bad press recently. As more and more individuals, their ranks swelled by discharged managers and retired executives with lumps of cash burning holes in their pocket, reach out for the elusive dream of being their own bosses, more are falling prey to the blandishments of the less reputable business brokers. Business brokers are only one source of leads to businesses to buy. Proceed with caution.

Another source of leads to businesses for sale is the business-opportunities ads in *The Wall Street Journal*, other news media, and trade and professional journals. Be careful. Some of those ads have been placed by business brokers dragging their own seines to catch potential buyers.

Most likely, however, the best source of leads to businesses for sale is the same one that outplacement specialists push so strongly to help their clients find new jobs. It's networking. Pursued vigorously, networking can turn up the most promising leads. An added attraction of this source—you won't be hotly chased as is often the case with brokers, franchisers, and franchise consultants. That doesn't mean, though, that you should exercise any less care when looking into the opportunity.

Don't get your hopes up that buying a company that's already in business eliminates your risks. For self-protection, you need two other key players: an expert independent accountant and an experienced acquisition attorney. However, they can only guide and advise. The final buying decision is a business one. Much of the work that goes with gathering the facts to reach well-founded decisions rests with you.

THE OVERLOOKED FACTOR— MARKET INFORMATION

Emphasis on "the numbers" and on the structure of the buy-sell agreement often overshadows the importance of gathering and interpreting market information. Such analyses are not in the areas of expertise of accountants and lawyers. The responsibility for studies of the market falls squarely on your shoulders.

A market analysis includes both the present position of the company and its outlook for the future. You need to study the current state of the market for the company's output, whether product or service—or a combination of both. You need to know the extent and nature of competition and factors that may have an impact on the company's market for the future. In some respects gathering market information resembles the steps you'd go through as a corporate strategic planner.

You need to know not only where the company has been and its current status, but also where it could—and should—be five years up the road. You have to assess the threats to reaching your goals for the company as well as the opportunities for profit. Threats can range from foreign, low-cost competitors suddenly blowing your doors off, to government decisions to run a new highway right through the center of company property.

You can obtain certain market information from the seller's internal records. You'll have to get the rest from outside sources. Entire books have been written on the details you need and the sources you can look to for help on market information. The purpose here is to get you to replace hunches, guesswork, and the seller's interest in painting a bright picture of his business with actual, hard-core facts.

The sources of financial information, both internal and external, should be mined by the expert accountant you must retain. Your lawyer should explore all the legalities of acquisition. He or she must also become totally familiar with the legalities which the company you seek to buy faces in the normal, and sometimes not so normal, course of its business. The attorney's job reaches far beyond merely structuring the buy-sell agreement.

Bear in mind, too, that all the psychic and psychological factors that you must account for before you start up a business of your own apply with equal force to buying a going concern. There are no shortcuts. There are no easy routes to becoming your own boss. *Caveat emptor*—Let the buyer beware—the Romans advised. Nowhere does that maxim apply more strongly than to buying a going concern.

THE FRANCHISE GAME

The literature available on franchising is extensive. Much of it is highly useful. The most valuable is published by the U.S. Department of Commerce. It issues updated handbooks and pamphlets covering the franchising scene. Before you take any steps at all in the direction of investing in a franchise, get a copy of *Franchise Opportunities Handbook*. It's available from the Government Printing Office in Washington, D.C. This 250-page handbook, prepared by the Department of Commerce, is an invaluable guide and source of information.

What do Coca-Cola, Mobil, Holiday Inns, and H&R Block have in common? Franchises. Franchising has become an integral and important part of the American business picture. All franchises generated an estimated $591 billion in sales in 1987, a substantial portion of the U.S. economy. Retail franchises account for more than 80 percent of those sales. Still, there are substantial revenues generated by service-to-business and business-to-business franchises. The high visibility of fast-food chains may have given you the idea that all franchises are oriented to the ultimate consumer. That's not the case.

Franchising goes back more than 100 years. Until recently, however, a "franchise" was held in somewhat less esteem by the general public than individually owned businesses or large corporations. That situation resulted in part from the promotional excesses that occurred in the 1950s and 1960s. So many people were burned, lost their lifetime savings, and remained indebted (or forced into bankruptcy) that, predictably, the government stepped in. The Federal Trade Commission and a number of states established stringent rules of disclosure for franchisers.

They have not killed off unscrupulous franchisers or franchise consultants completely. Neither the FTC nor the states afford complete before- or after-the-fact protection. But studying the rules carefully, along with the franchise agreement itself, has contributed to deterring the unbounded enthusiasm that even the most intelligent people let sway their investment decisions.

Does that mean that franchises are risk-free? Positively not. Indeed, you can make a case that investing in a franchise is just as risky as your other two options to become your own boss. There are two main elements of risk: one is that the franchiser may be poorly run; the other is that you may not be able to manage that kind of business properly.

In the end there are no substitutes for going through the same steps to determine if you're the right type to be a business owner. Begin your evaluation with yourself, just as you would with a start-up or buying an ongoing business. You must also go through the tricky task of choosing the type of business most suited to you. After all, a franchise is your own business.

It is true that as a franchisee you'd be less free to make all your own decisions. You can't tear down the golden arches should you decide that you'd prefer a hedgerow of totem poles at the entrance. You may also be restricted to when, where, and how to obtain certain supplies, how you keep your books, and other details of managing the business.

Offsetting those disadvantages, though, you do have track records of experience behind your franchise. And the management "supervision" given you by the franchiser is, except with a brand-new one, experience-based.

You can follow standard routines which will afford you some protection against the charlatans and crooks who do from time to time invade the franchising field. Investigating the franchiser is an early step. Every kind of franchiser has competitors, particularly the blue chips. Once you've chosen the kind of business you are best suited to be in, "kick tires" among the franchisers offering the opportunities.

Pick several franchisers. An FTC regulation requires them to give you disclosure statements. If they aren't included in the materials given you, the yellow flag is snapping in the breeze signaling caution. Remember that you're playing the selling game with professionals and they have the edge; they're experts in sales techniques.

They may use "negative selling" to whet your appetite for making a deal. Of course, they have other prospective franchisees to whom they can turn if you won't jump at closing the deal. When they appear reticent about certain details, remember that they may be using negative selling. You'll never know for sure. Don't give in to that pressure.

Nothing should deter you from asking for the disclosure statement. It will cover detailed information on twenty different areas, any one of which may influence your decision to invest. You can get a list of items that must be included in a disclosure statement from the Federal Trade Commission. Compare actual statements you receive with the FTC's guidelines. Have an attorney review and compare them, too. Also, compare one franchiser's disclosure statement against another's.

Then, start verifying the information the statement contains by contacting several, at least three, of the franchisees listed in the disclosure statement. Don't confine yourself to those recommended by the franchiser. You can further protect yourself by asking the franchiser to substantiate any earnings claims made for franchises, whether written, displayed, or given orally. FTC rules require franchisers to do so on request. Some states require substantiation of such claims whether you ask for it or not.

Getting professional reviews

When you get the franchiser's earnings statements, have them reviewed by an accountant or other financial professional. You want to be sure that the franchiser is in sound financial condition so it can carry out its obligations to you and other franchisees.

You need a lawyer who is expert in the franchising field. These days lawyers are as specialized as doctors. Don't rely on your brother-in-law or a friend who may be fine for wills, estates, or real estate closings. Get a lawyer who practices in the field.

You have certain legal rights under federal law as a prospective franchisee. They are given to you by FTC trade regulations and rules. Get them under your belt before you even start your search. Make sure, as you go through the process of seeking out the right kind of franchise for you, that you exercise every single right that's yours.

Bear in mind that the burden of investigation is still on you. No federal agency has reviewed, much less approved, the disclosure statements or the franchise agreements. If a violation of federal or state law occurs, you can report it to the FTC, but that's like locking the barn door after the horse has been stolen. Even though the FTC is authorized to seek redress for injured parties, it is not required to do so. Should you need to get relief from any document you sign or commitment you make, you may have to get it through a private lawyer—one more reason you should have one on board right from the start.

In addition to evaluating yourself and the franchiser, you must study the market. Despite the professed and proferred expertise of the franchiser in connection with market knowledge, you must go through the same steps of gathering market information as you would if you were starting up a business or buying a going concern.

Franchising is a term from the French that originally meant "to be free from servitude." It's currently being used to denote opportunity to own one's own business even if inexperienced and lacking adequate capital. You may be looking upon the exciting prospect of having a business of your own as a route to freedom. Be sure you do not confuse the "free" with the free and easy.

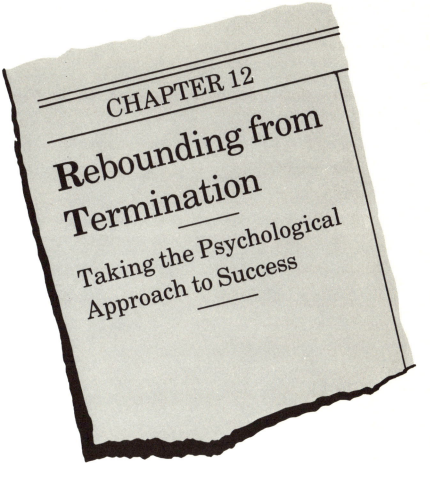

CHAPTER 12

Rebounding from Termination

Taking the Psychological Approach to Success

ALL the advice in the world on starting your own business or conducting a successful job hunt or taking advantage of outplacement services won't help you one whit if you're not ready to help yourself.

Some people get destroyed by the firing process; others get energized by it. It's not easy to become a member of that second group. It's not easy to look at a pink slip and see an opportunity . . . to be on the receiving end of a termination lecture and hear a new chance for success ring in your ears.

That's just what you should be seeing and hearing. If you approach termination with the right mindset, that is what you will see and hear. Your dismissal will become an opportunity to tackle some of those things you've often promised yourself you'd do "someday" but that you've never been able to try. An opportunity to move in different directions, to accept invigorating challenges, to explore exciting career paths.

You may have been operating on cruise control in your personal comfort zone. The regimented world of the corporation may have been stultifying to your personal and professional growth. You may have been programmed to rush through the rat race without caring where that final corridor would lead. You may have been cheating yourself out of achieving all that you can achieve. And you *can* achieve.

You're at the stage in your professional life when

you deserve a chance to sit back, put your feet up, jiggle the ice in your drink, and reflect on just where you've been, where you're headed, and, most important, where you want to end up.

YA GOTTA BELIEVE

Norman Vincent Peale, famed minister and best-known proponent of positive thinking, describes the power you possess to take charge of your life this way: "If there is literally enough force in you to blow up the greatest city in the world, there is also literally enough power in you to overcome every obstacle in your life." If you think that starting a new career looms over you like some insurmountable Mount Everest, remember that you have within you the levers to pry any obstacles out of the way.

Tug McGraw was the ace reliever of baseball's New York Mets when they struggled from behind to win the National League pennant and go the distance before losing the 1973 World Series. McGraw made "Ya gotta believe" a kind of Norman Vincent Peale sports slogan. It carried the same type of weight in urging his teammates to their ultimate triumph as did Sam Houston's memorable war cry "Remember the Alamo" for the victory his ragtag army of Texans posted over the infamous Santa Anna at the Battle of San Jacinto. Norman Vincent Peale, Tug McGraw, and Sam Houston (as mixed a bag of characters whose exhortations have ever been collectively cited in two paragraphs) never promised anyone that victory would be easy—only that it would be worth the effort.

You're among the growing number of managers who have suffered, perhaps still suffer, severe trauma from being discharged, or facing its threat. Many of those individuals have experienced depression, loss of hope, worthlessness, and bitterness despite the fact that what happened to them occurred through no fault of their own.

One such individual, who claims he went through every level of despair even to the final edge of suicide, tells this story.

"There exists an infinity of ways to structure self-rescue from such depths. One to which I was introduced by my father and which both he and I used frequently on pleasant as well as unpleasant occasions was the mental creation of a 'Board of Directors' or mentors in our daily lives.

"We could put anyone on our Boards that we liked. Mine had a variety, from Jesus Christ through George Washington, Abraham Lincoln, and my father, after he passed away. The trick is to engage them in serious conversations on any subject on which help is needed.

"One day, after about two months of self-castigation on my job loss, one of my mentors asked me: 'Well, are you going to kill yourself or aren't you?' The question shook me up a bit. I thought about it seriously and then answered my inner leader, 'No, I guess I'm not. I guess maybe I don't have the courage to do that.'

"The unflappable mentor then said, 'Well, if you're sure you've made that decision, let me ask you, do you want to go on living in this gloom and doom?' I didn't have to think about that one very long. 'No,' I shouted. Perhaps facing an ultimatum is a catharsis that is sometimes required to remedy desperate situations.

"My son reminded me of another relevant incident. He had called me from college to say that school just wasn't for him. When I had found him crushed by what seemed to him such a great failure on his part to me and to his fellow students, I told him: 'You would not worry so much about what other people think of you if you knew how seldom they do.' He reminded me of that when my own despair developed. Now I know what I said to him applied with equal force to me.

"I have learned that we must take command of ourselves first of all—of our innermost thinking and reacting. None of this can be forced or only surface-deep or it will be worthless; worse than worthless—it will destroy us if we use it falsely. Many people have tried across the centuries of history to get across one simple message: 'You can if you think you can.' But *you* have to ask, *you* have to seek, *you* have to do."

Some years ago an advertising manager of a small company was sent on a mission to persuade the famous merchant James Cash Penney to allow his picture and endorsement to be used in an advertising campaign. Then age eighty-five, honorary Chairman of J.C. Penney & Company and still going to his office each day, Penney listened, approved the quotes in the copy, and later posed for a formal portrait to be used in the ad.

Upon returning to his office, the manager was asked if Mr. Penney had agreed to the imposition. "Of course he did," the ad manager replied with certainty. "I expected him to."

Both the innovative father and the confident ad manager had the right idea. There are no limits to an individual's potential except self-imposed ones. Setting real goals—not just wishes or hopes—is an essential ingredient for you, or anyone else, in benefiting from the rule of expectations. You cannot achieve anything in life without expecting to achieve it. Most individuals are defeated not because they don't try, but because they don't expect to achieve.

You will achieve out there in the world at large just what you expect to achieve. But you can also expect this: if you go forth with a chip on each shoulder, you will encounter an entire world anxious to oblige you by knocking them off. So the first bit of psychology to adhere to in your job search is to work to negate certain negative reactions.

REACTIONS TO AVOID

You may not be able to avoid actual feelings like anger, disbelief, and self-pity even after you apply some of the combat techniques you'll see spelled out later in this chapter. But you can avoid some of the reactions that go with those negative emotions.

Sure you're angry. But don't get loud and abusive or make a scene. Don't threaten to sue or go to the media. Don't bad-mouth anyone to anyone. This is especially true of those you worked with, including secretaries and staff. They can turn into your best bets for future job leads. Also, some individuals interviewed reported that their former employers had called them back for special, temporary consulting assignments after termination, something that would have never happened if they had left on less than cordial terms.

Even if you can't believe this is happening to you, take it with a stiff upper lip. No whining about how unfair it is or how you don't deserve to be shafted like this. Of course you don't, but you were. Can the self-pity! You're not so badly off. If you indulge in feeling sorry for yourself, you can travel right down the chute to depression, withdrawal, inertia—absolutely the worse reactions for a job seeker who should be marshalling all his or her energies into the job search.

There are some other emotional reactions that if you can't exorcise, you can at least recognize and try to prevent from hampering that search. Don't be embarrassed by your predicament or take a firing personally. Don't lie to yourself or fabricate excuses. Don't clam up or make like an ostrich. Face it. It won't go away no matter how much you deny it. If you totally bury your feelings during the immediate post-termination period, you might make the situation appear more placid then, but it could churn up waves of future psychological problems. You can and should speak with many people about your situation, but in a rational, logical manner.

Says one manager who has been through it and rebounded: "It's good to talk about it. Having gone through it, I never want to lose it. But I never want to have to experience it again."

Says another: "People who get fired and keep it to themselves are missing such a rich experience. . . . they're cheating themselves."

It's easy to pontificate about how you shouldn't react. It's a little harder working up a positive mental frame of reference for how you should. As you embark on the adventure of building another career, keep in mind these pearls from Henry David Thoreau: "If you have built castles in the air, your work need not be lost; there is where they should be. Now put foundations under them." For foundation layers, try some of these "rebound reactions" for starters.

REACTIONS YOU DO WANT TO CULTIVATE

Rebound Reaction #1: "Getting fired happens to the best of individuals, so it's no disgrace that it happened to me." Bob McCarthy, who counsels corporations on termination programs, came up with an idea to start a Golden Ax Hall of Fame. Think about some of your compadres in cutting. There's no shame to be included among these names of fame.

Winston Churchill was fired as first lord of the Admiralty. Ben Franklin lost one job for being a wastrel. David Letterman washed out as a weatherman. Chrysler's Lee Iaccoca may one day run for president, but he was driven from his job at Ford. Tack a golden plaque on your mental wall, give an Arnie Palmer hitch to your pants, and start in on the first day of the rest of your life—which happens to be today.

Rebound Reaction #2: "I'm positive there is a better job out there just waiting for me to grab it." A University of Michigan study on job-loss trauma found that a person's beliefs about the chances of finding new employment stimulate job-seeking behavior and lead to more frequent and intensive efforts to find a job. Throw your heart into the job-seeking ring and your body will automatically follow.

Repeat Tug McGraw's famous words, "Ya gotta believe." When you do believe strongly enough in your future job chances, and expect fully to win a new job, these twin divining rods become a self-fulfilling prophecy.

Rebound Reaction #3: "Getting fired IS NOT a sign of incompetence on my part." In truth, incompetents don't reach responsible middle-management positions as you did in the first place. Talented and capable people are being fired right and left, even after they rack up good results.

One senior technical-writing manager, whose salary came in each year at the high five-figure level, had lightning strike twice. Some years ago he was bounced from his job with a major publishing company which decided to fold the magazine of which he was editor. More recently his job in a public relations position was eliminated when the giant electrical-product firm which employed him decided to eliminate the entire function.

"But I knew that my work was good in both instances," this manager insisted. "We'd been profitable, got excellent ink and much praise from the media, so I knew it wasn't me, or my fault. I knew it and I believed it and that's one reason why, when I told a client company of my circumstances, they made me an immediate offer—at higher pay."

In today's turbulent economy, people and positions are at risk no matter what. One job seeker had it right when he explained, "I just happened to be in the wrong place at the wrong time."

At the same time, don't ignore what a dismissal may tell you about yourself or your position. If you did contribute in some way to your downfall, no matter how inadvertently, find out what it was so you can correct it next time around. Maybe this termination is telling you something about your industry/function/position. Most people instinctively reach out for a similar job in the same industry. You may be totally wrong to take that approach. The industry may be dying, your function may be changing, the position you held may not have maximized your assets—and now you can shape the direction of your search with that insight.

Rebound Reaction #4: "I suppose the actual dismissal probably could have been handled worse than it was." Sure it could. One forty-year veteran was given the gate in a coffee shop and then told not to go back to the office. Another manager was canned the day after his cancer tests came back positive. A third got a call at home from his boss on Friday and was told to "take Monday off." He first thought he was being given another vacation day. Then his boss continued, "By the way, come in today and clear out your desk. And don't try to come into the building again. The guards have already been told that it's off limits to you."

Callous and cruel? Sure. And stupid, too. Your rebound reaction to any similar dismissal? You're lucky to be out from under an executive who treats individuals in that manner. If he would dismiss a person in that way, there's no telling what else he might do to you behind your back. Your only misfortune was not to have beaten such a boss to the punch and taken yourself out of that ring years before. At that company, you had no "castle in the air," and no foundation to build for it.

Rebound Reaction #5: "The poor suckers I left behind are in even worse shape than I am." The survivor syndrome can weigh more heavily on a manager's psyche than even the burden of unemployment. Anxiety and insecurity abound. They're constantly looking over their shoulders, walking on eggshells. They have to do more with less, all the while sadly surveying the empty desks of former comrades who were bayoneted into oblivion.

You might also take some vicarious pleasure from the fact that your loss is the company's loss as well. It will have to deal with some tough psychological problems, just as you will. Top management is forced to confront questions like:

- How do we get those survivors to forget the terminations and concentrate on their jobs?
- How do we overcome the alienation and enthusiasm drop in those remaining?
- How do we reassure and retain star performers who are upset by the turmoil?
- How do we put the kibosh on the morale-sapping rumor mill?
- How do we replace the knowledge files contained in the heads of the departing managers, ranging from competitor intelligence to product cycles?

One interviewee said about current work at his former employer: "Oh, the job is getting done but not as expertly nor as timely. The corporation will get along okay without us—all companies have momentum. They'll pay a price in competitiveness, though, several years down the line."

Rebound Reaction #6: "I'm still young enough and healthy enough and talented enough to seize this opportunity to turn a career interruption into a dream realization." Indeed, this is your chance to shuck the negatives of the old job and accept a whole different set of energizing challenges from a new one. The margin between what you might naturally do and what you *can* do is so great that even a little action or a little initiative on your part promises to bring results that until now you may not have dared to dream about.

What are you waiting for? Begin to prepare for that challenge by boldly confronting those disturbing emotions that you're feeling.

RUNNING THE GAMUT OF FEELINGS

"I'll never get over the rejection. Never."

That wasn't the sigh of a star-struck teenager having been shot down on a big prom date. It was the reaction of an experienced and battle-hardened manager who was blown out of his job by a downsizing howitzer.

The personal agonies suffered by displaced managers run the emotional gamut from grief, fear, and shock, to disbelief, anger, and self-pity; from panic, terror, and depression to shame, anxiety, and outright hostility; from frustration and resentment to denial and withdrawal. And more!

Here are some typical descriptions:

- "It hit me like a ton of bricks. I was in a state of shock. And I was gone. Just like that. Poof."
- "I couldn't believe it. Took twenty-one years to build up a career and ten minutes to tear it down."
- "I was caught totally off guard. How could something like this happen in five minutes?"
- "All those years just went down the drain . . . like a light being turned off."

Every one of these quotations came from individuals who have been tested in the crucible of firing. Every one is now happily racing along a new career track. Yet, they've found no easy way to erase those feelings. In fact, it's been better instead for them—and for you—to get them out in the open. Psychologists say "make written lists" as that activity in itself has therapeutic value. Write all your feelings down. Then take each one and go one-on-one with it.

One especially bitter emotional pill for the long-term manager to swallow is the utter disregard for loyalty that many terminations reflect. Face it—the day of the good soldier is gone. Dismissed managers are being forced to approach their employment more in terms of a job than a career.

Declining loyalty on both sides of the employer/employee equation (as you saw in Chapter 2) has shattered the fragile bonds that formerly bound those sides. The "Me first" syndrome has run rampant, to the detriment of all.

Said one employed former job hunter: "If I, the manager, know I have security and a career, I can take the long view, even if I'm only a toiler in the vineyard. But if I don't have that security, I can't put the company's interests before my own. That's the concept being bred in managers today. And it's like a contagious disease being passed by those managers who are terminated to their new places of employment."

High-profile executives as diverse as Red Auerbach of the Boston Celtics and Chrysler's Iaccoca have their thoughts on the subject.

Auerbach: "I really believe that loyalty is a two-way street. Unfortunately, in most cases, business executives expect loyalty from employees, but are very reluctant to give loyalty."

Iaccoca: "When we finally held the victory parade, a lot of our soldiers were missing." [So were the lieutenants.]

Psychologically you must first of all realize that you are going to take a ride on an emotional roller coaster during the post-dismissal period. Second, you mustn't let those emotions prevent you from acting. For example, shame is one of the biggest deterrents to positive networking. Third, you should recognize that many of the emotions are self-imposed. Try objectivity and perspective. Finally, it's imperative that you develop a personal program to combat the negative feelings that may be holding you back and to tap the positive emotions to propel you forward. Here are some weapons.

ENTERING THE COMBAT ZONE

Count your blessings. You've heard that one since you were a little kid. Now it's more pertinent than ever. Make a list, especially of the intangible ones. A major national survey probed for Americans' definition of success. The top four named were:

- Being a good parent
- Having a happy marriage
- Having a good relationship with another person
- Having friends who respect you

Says nothing about earning big bucks or having fancy job titles, does it?

Stay in control. One of the biggest complaints of displaced managers is that they feel swept along by fate, no longer in control of their own destinies. That's why it's important to create a job-search system and stick to it. You really do control your future if you've planned how to make it come to pass. Don't surrender control to employment agencies, counselors, even friends.

And don't let your job search take control of you. One manager spent a lot of spare time working with the handicapped. When he was dismissed, he contemplated dropping that charity work and concentrating solely on his job search. After considerable mental wrestling, he rejected that path. In fact, continuing that work made him that much more aware of just how fortunate he really was.

Maintain your self-esteem. Having rarely suffered defeat as you climbed the corporate ladder, a pink slip can deal a devastating right hook to your feeling of personal worth. Concentrate on the first part of that idea. Whenever a doubt arises in your mind, confront it with one of your achievements. You have been successful. It was no accident. You worked hard to get where you were. You can do it again. Remember that your personal identity is not circumscribed by your job. You are your own person. Take good, hard second looks at yourself. They usually reveal that the task you may initially have thought impossible is quite possible after all.

Boost your feelings of self-worth. The almighty "they" of the faceless corporate structure may have decided you're not worth keeping. You know better. You are unique, an individual with your own history of accomplishments and records. Review them. Accept the positive; downplay the negative. Now is not the time to be self-critical. Don't compare yourself to others or diminish your own achievements by setting them against those of others. Listen to your Thomas Magnum-like inner voice. It will reassure you when outside voices are tearing you down.

Don't overlook personal as well as professional highlights in your past. Think about all the times you helped others when nobody else could—or would.

Examine your feelings objectively. Write down the negative ones, and fire away at them. Then cut them loose. Take a specific one, like anxiety. It's difficult to avoid because it deals with the unknown, an apprehension about the anticipation of danger or problems. If you can't avoid, use it. Treat it like stage fright, and tap it to make you concentrate harder, prepare better, get the adrenaline pumping. Identify previous transitions in your life, focus on how you dealt with them, evaluate the elements of satisfaction they produced. Those are known. Plug them into future expectations, and the unknown becomes a little less imposing.

Play the devil's advocate. Get your buried fears out in the open. Conduct your own "shrink" session (charge yourself 85 bucks and stretch out on a couch if you want). Ask yourself what's the very worst that could happen. You become a bag person. Go to debtor's prison. Kids go hungry. Pretty ludicrous, right? So instead ask yourself, "What can I do to react positively to a bad situation?" Now you're on the right track. Relax. Avoid compulsive activity. Don't fling yourself into a frenzy. Don't hit the streets the day after your dismissal.

Take a look at people who seem to do things with minimum effort. When doing so, they develop maximum power. Visualize, when you can, Joe DiMaggio, who loped apparently effortlessly after towering flies in Yankee Stadium. Or the Cardinals' Ozzie Smith who swoops, scoops, and throws to first base with grace, ease, and power.

Don't press. Don't overtry. Don't get tense. Relax. James Baker, chief executive officer of Arvin Industries, is a master of always appearing at ease. Some time back, at Arvin's picnic to celebrate its seventy-five years in business, Baker was besieged by people clamoring for his attention as he escorted the guests of honor to their car. Without apparently missing a step as he guided the guests, he quietly gave each interrupting individual the appearance of attention to their needs with a quiet word, a smile, or a nod of his head. A study in the most efficient use of practical ease, Baker releases maximum power. He practices its use. You can too.

And most importantly, keep communicating. Don't isolate. Take your cue from Roger Schultz.

TAKING THE WORLD BY STORM

You'll recall Schultz, whom you first met back in Chapter 2. He began his recovery from a stormy dismissal in the middle of a tempest. He and twenty-five others in his corporate function had received "the word" on the Friday morning when infamous Hurricane Gloria struck the Northeast. Schultz had to drive home through torrential rains, cutting through parking lots and taking other detours to avoid the deepest pockets of water on flooded streets.

He had to make decisions whether to keep driving or abandon his car and hike. That dangerous exercise kept his mind occupied and may have had therapeutic effects. Suffice it to say, when your very life is at stake, there's little chance to become immediately depressed about a job loss. However, courting danger is not recommended to combat depression. Activity is.

When Roger finally arrived home, though, the chore of telling his wife and coping with her bitter reaction to his former employer caused him to "reach for a bottle of Glenlivet." That, he says, propped him up for the weekend. On Monday morning, however, he immediately began to make the phone wires hum to others in his group who'd been let go. They quickly organized a get-together which effectively functioned as a support group—much like those which some outplacement firms and services like HELP WANTED and 40+ weld together.

This association with others turned into immense help for Schultz and other members on two counts:

1. The gatherings caused group members to turn outward rather than retreat as they worked together to help each other

2. During their meetings they shared information and "What do we do?" planning ideas—a practical exercise as well as a catharsis for each member.

One specific activity which the group organized was asking a CPA to answer questions about how to start up a business. Schultz reports that the vast majority of the group were experiencing "sour tastes" from working for a heartless giant corporation. They were, Schultz says, determined to make their own breaks in the future rather than depend on a "legal person," a corporation. This became a group, as well as an individual, objective for many members.

In addition, the group members personally circulated among friends, acquaintances, and family members both for psychological support and for practical opportunities. It's clear that the sharing of experiences, thoughts, objectives, goals and working to help others, as well as yourself, provides a far more permanent "pick-me-up" than even the best bottle of Glenlivet. It reinforces the knowledge that you're not alone, that there are others in the same boat, and that such dismissals come about through no fault of your own.

Keep those thoughts foremost in your mind. They are keys to your success in anything which you tackle in the future. You gain positive reinforcement from contact with other people. Never try to bear your burdens alone. No person can be an island in this world and survive, much less thrive.

Roger Schultz was, in fact, offered a good job with another major corporation. In the end he rejected it and is now busily engaged in filling freelance writing assignments. He has coauthored one book and has planned another.

Schultz attributes a good share of his attitude turnaround to the support he received from his group. When asked just before this book went to press how things were going, he laughed and said, "No problems." He's a happy man—and for anyone, anyone at all, what more can you ask?

Coping with the Emotions of Others

Once you've dealt with your own feelings, you've got some other people and their feelings to deal with. The first is your family. Then there are the colleagues you're leaving behind, your friends and neighbors, and the network participants you hope to enlist in your search. That University of Michigan study done on the trauma of job loss concluded that psychological damage is much more severe than economic and that the best medicine is to find a replacement position quickly. Not exactly startling findings.

It also discovered that victims can be so demoralized that they are prevented from conducting an effective job search, and that the second most important boost (after getting another job) is the social support from loved ones and friends to help maintain confidence and handle the normal rejection and failure surrounding job hunting.

Everyone involved in counseling terminated individuals and those who have been through the experience themselves agrees that making each member of the family a partner in all phases of the process is a requisite for post-termination peace of mind.

Whatever you do, don't fall into the trap one fired manager did when he refused to discuss any aspect of his termination with his family for six months after the ax fell. He finally admitted—to himself and them—that it was the biggest mistake he could have made. Sharing emotions can be an indispensable source of sustenance in troubled times.

Put together a group counseling session of your own. Help your spouse and children to identify their feelings and forebodings, and to express them. Emphasize the importance of communicating, sharing, and viewing things objectively. Create a framework for everyone to contribute, with long- and short-term goals for both personal and group satisfaction.

Go through a structured exercise to clarify everyone's position, what exactly are the losses (and gains), what each person needs to know, and what actions they need to take. Develop a concrete plan for how each person should react and interact. Identify means for coping and developing a positive attitude. Expose frustrations and offer options.

All this will have a twofold benefit. Your partners in this tough process will feel better, and you will feel better knowing that. You won't have to worry about them as you focus your efforts on solving your main problem—finding a new job.

Use the same personal approach with the people you are leaving at work. Whatever you do, don't burn any bridges. Don't let any feelings of resentment or anger lead you into saying or doing something you'll later regret. Tie up all loose ends, finish projects, help with status reports—do anything you can to leave a good taste in everyone's mouths. Don't stop there. Keep in touch. Remember your networking lessons.

In fact, you can draw psychological aid as well as practical help from your business network contacts. One out-of-work ex-manager told this story:

"During my first month out of work I was okay. Too busy to get upset. There was so much to do, so many loose ends to tie up. I really had no time to get depressed.

"Then it hit me. I'd always been very active, and now I had to sit around and wait for the phone to ring. I hated it. The one thing that really helped to get me through was the outpouring of positive response from those I had contacted about work.

"It wasn't only the nice things they said about my past accomplishments or the compliments on my résumé. Why, a printer I know set the type for my résumé for nothing. And a customer I never met face-to-face when I was employed, who I had only talked with on the phone, she called the vice-president of her company to ask if there were any openings for me.

"What a great morale booster. I began to feel that my old employer had made a bad mistake when he let me go. It was a great feeling."

Friends and neighbors can pose communication problems for the terminated too. Some neighbors become not so neighborly. "They treated me like I had cancer or something," complained one ex-manager.

Again, get your "objective" glasses on. Look at it from their perspective. They may feel as badly as you do about your situation, but they don't know how to react, don't know what to say, or which subjects you might be touchy about. The solution? Tell them. You bring it up. Talk about it openly and with a sense of humor. Don't always be in your "job search" mode. Show them you are still the same friend or neighbor you were while employed.

One manager said that when he and his wife went to parties shortly after he was fired, she would come out with, "Say, Bob has lost his job. Has anyone seen it? Maybe we should look for it under the table or behind that chair." Her gutsy handling of a stressful situation accomplished many useful things. She relaxed her husband, and her friends, completely sweeping away a potential pall over the proceedings should the bad news seep slowly out. Not to be overlooked: getting the word out is part of networking.

Don Sweet, the Hawkins Associates counselor, injects his own brand of humor into the situation. "Look at it this way," says Sweet. "If you're on a plane and want some peace and quiet, what better conversation squelcher than 'I'm so-and-so and I really need a job.' That short response can sure pull the plug on a long conversation."

STRESS—THE UNWANTED NEIGHBOR

Stress is a constant companion for most middle managers, and it usually doesn't terminate with a termination. If anything, it intensifies.

Drs. Thomas H. Holmes and Richard H. Rahe, whose work was mentioned in Chapter 3, developed a way to measure stressful events in an individual's life. The Holmes Readjustment Scale gives a rating to forty-two stressful life changes. "Fired at work" and "retirement" are both in the top ten, followed closely by "business adjustment," "change in finances," and "change to different work."

You don't have to have someone tell you that you're under stress after losing your job. You know some of the signs:

- Headaches, stomach and/or back pains
- Trouble sleeping, worried by business or financial demands
- Loss of appetite, skipping meals
- Business considerations dominate thinking
- Emotions tougher to keep under control

In fact, the more successful you've been prior to termination, the more likely it is that stress will continue to follow you around and make things more difficult for you afterward.

How to beat stress? First, you should identify stress patterns and be prepared to respond with positive alternatives. For example, if you still feel fatigued after eight hours of bed rest, a sign of stress, take a brisk walk, a positive response. Second, you should recognize that stress is an internal mechanism by which your body and mind mobilize energy for coping with change and challenge.

Ever jumped when a horn honked unexpectedly? The noise exerts stress, and your jump was your mind mobilizing your body to react, perhaps to take flight. And third, you should be determined to take advantage of personal stressful reactions to identify problems, strengthen your defenses, sharpen your resolve, and stimulate yourself to greater efforts.

Conduct a stress audit of yourself. What particular situations and actions cause you stress? How can you either turn them to your advantage or avoid them? To turn down your personal stress level, you might consider:

- Exercise (breathing programs and neck movements)
- Imagery (pretending the cause of your tension is a tennis ball and you're about to blast it with your best forehand)
- Physical outlets (home carpentry, lawn work, car repair)
- Dietary changes, since a body under stress may be hypersensitive to certain foods (e.g., alcohol and sweets may bring on sluggishness)
- Special acts (putting your stress on ice by talking into a tape, yelling, complaining, getting negative feelings off your chest; then putting that tape in the freezer, or even better, in the garbage).

Bear in mind that you should use the forces of stress to propel you into positive reactions. Dr. Hans Selye, noted for his studies and writings about stress, says: "Don't be afraid to enjoy the stress of a full life nor be too naïve to think you can do without some intelligent thinking and planning. Man should not try to avoid stress any more than he would shun food, love or exercise."

THINGS ARE LOOKING UP

No matter how much stress you're under, looking on the bright side of situations will always help.

Famous baseball announcer Vin Scully is credited with the quote that: "Statistics are used by baseball fans in much the same way a drunk leans against a lamp-post; it's there more for support than enlightenment."

There are more and more statistics beginning to emerge out there that support a good deal of hope for the out-of-work manager.

The Bureau of Labor Statistics weighs in with these rosy figures:

- The total number of executive, managerial and administrative jobs in public and private sectors of the United States economy has actually grown by 2.8 million in the 1980s.
- Between 1984 and 1995, such positions will increase by 22 percent, led by business and professional services.
- Job openings for manufacturing managers and administrators will grow by 200,000 by 1995.

The nationally recognized Hudson Institute think tank predicts that by the year 2000, there will be 3.8 million new managerial positions, 5.8 million new professional and technical openings, and 3.6 million new sales and marketing jobs.

There's more. The BLS also says that 50 percent of displaced workers make more on their new jobs. Outplacement firms peg that percentage even higher. Reports have it that twenty-three of twenty-five terminated Union Carbide managers making between $50,000 and $100,000 found positions that met their objectives after receiving outplacement.

Says a newly hired former job seeker: "To put it crassly, I drove a Volkswagon to work at my old job. Now I drive a Seville."

One management recruiter said: "We have more demand for middle managers than ever before."

Another: "It's a seller's market for managers."

New attitudes are emerging toward out-of-work and over forty managers among hiring firms. Higher percentages of new employees in corporations are coming from that experienced group. A major surveyer of the job market scene reported that the new "first in line to be hired" was the manager over forty-four, making around $50,000, who had at least two previous jobs.

New trends are picking up steam. Companies are getting tired of the fast-track younger managers using them as stepping-stones for career growth. Stability and experience are back in vogue.

Competitiveness is the watchword of the day in all sectors of American business. The introduction of new products, new services, new technologies—the kind of innovation that creates competitive advantage—will create more areas for companies to manage. That's good news for the skilled professional managerial types caught in the threshing machine of downsizing.

Even the trend toward downsizing itself has contributed new management opportunities. The slashing of internal staff has produced a two-tier system with a concurrent need for more external services, which can be provided by experienced managers going into business for themselves, or going to work for one of the contractors that provide the services.

The truth is, you are needed. "They" need you. The problem is to go out there and find "them." If you've been paying attention, you should be ready to go out there and grab your personal brass ring.

CHAPTER 13

Tales of Triumph

This Is the First Day of the Rest of Your Life

PROOF.

If it's really true that the plight of the dismissed manager can be turned into the light of a new career, where's the hard-core evidence?

If all the practical suggestions and psychological ploys you've read about here really work, you may utter the old Missouri standby "Show me!"

That's what the brief case histories in this chapter are designed to do. Show you that other managers in your position have hitched up their pants and pushed on to greater rewards. Show you that disemployment needn't be a curse, but can be turned into a blessing. Show you that happy endings do occur in real life, and that despite your loss there are extraordinary gains out there waiting for you to pursue them.

The stories you will read here are true. "Only the names and dates have been changed to protect the innocent." You'll find a variety of situations explained and an equal diversity of conclusions reached. The bottom line in each is that what began as a termination tempest turned into a sunrise opportunity that brought on brighter days for each of the dismissed managers whose stories are revealed here.

Some of these managers were caught in the downsizing thresher; some fell from grace due to old-fashioned politics. For some the experience was painfully unexpected, for others less shocking but no less depressing.

The rebound time for some was very short, for others a lengthy struggle.

The results of these cases vary in measure, but not in the "bottom line." All these ex-managers have succeeded in one form or another. Some got better jobs, higher positions, bigger paychecks. Others "found" themselves, got involved in activities that made them "happier than they'd ever been."

THE SECOND TIME AROUND

Practice makes perfect. That's at least one inference you could draw from Jim Turner's experiences when the chief executive of the giant firm for which he worked ordered his minions to lower the boom on management ranks. This wasn't the first time Jim had been caught in a restructuring. "Yeah, it was the second time around for me," Turner explained. "I'd been caught in the termination trap only two years before I got cut down this time. It was another giant company, though a different line of business. I'd invested twelve years of my life there and another two years at the new company when the ax fell again."

How did it feel when the T-word came along for the second time? "There's an immediate down reaction. No question. It was just as bad the second time as the first. One of the things I had going for me, though, was the fact that in both instances my whole area of responsibility was eliminated. In both cases my department had an excellent track record. So, I knew that getting let go *wasn't my fault*. It was the result of a high-level decision to reduce head count by eliminating my function.

"What really irks me is that my last company doesn't save a dime," continued Jim bitterly, "because they're spending it by hiring outside contractors to get the work done."

What was the source of his new job? "What everyone says about networking is true. I was working very closely with one of our clients. I knew they liked my work and I cultivated the people at that company, as well as letting others know what I did and how I was doing. I made myself thoroughly familiar with the client's product lines, with the company, and with new product planning. I did that not because I was afraid I might lose my job. I did that because that enabled me do my job better.

"And when I did get the word that our department was being eliminated, I felt confident that I could retain the billing if I took a job elsewhere."

And what was the outcome? "When I told the client company what was happening at the outfit where I was working, they made me an immediate offer. It's true that during the second time being spun off the merry-go-round I was luckier than the first. My severance date was October 31. I went to work for my current employer November 2."

What about benefits from the former employer? "Mine weren't very good. After all I'd only been there for two years. Some of the others got generous severance packages because they'd spent their whole lives there. The company did give me outplacement and I took it even though I already had the other offer which, incidentally, was in the high five figures, *a better salary than I'd been making*. I went through outplacement mostly for future reference. I thought it was okay but it could have been better. The program was geared for a lot of people, and there were only three or four of us at that location.

"Look, I'm fifty-four years old, married, two children, one in college. When you get there you've got both age and salary against you. You're making too much for many companies to want to match. I came out of the whole thing very well." Turner waxed enthusiastic. "I'm making more money. I'm working in a much smaller company where I get immediate decisions because there's

not as many layers of approval as there were at the outfits where I worked before. I'm now very happy with the
outcome."

Advice for others from Turner: "I've got to stress the
importance of follow-up and follow-through. Some people will think I was just lucky. I think it's more than
that. I *worked on* those relationships with clients. When
you work closely with others—clients, vendors, and almost anyone you come into contact with—that's part of
networking and you get better results in case of a job
loss. The company that fired me wasn't exactly downsizing when it cut out my department. It just decided to
get the work done in another way.

"I felt as secure there before the bad news hit as I've
felt anywhere. Networking isn't just a defensive measure, but it sure has that just-in-case aspect to it. It has
paid off in ways I've never even thought of. When you've
established a track record with people within your company, outside your company, and with those you may
not now or even have any business relationship with,
it'll pay off. It sure did for me."

ONLY ROOM FOR ONE

Dale Drummond was set, or so he thought. With a legal
background and over ten years with the same boss in
the same department, it seemed only a matter of time
before he ascended to the throne he sought.

Then came the department head's retirement, and
the coronation. Only the crown was placed on a newcom-
er's head. Not only did Dale lose out on the promotion,
but the new boss wanted to bring in his own people to
fill those important backup slots. Drummond was ban-
ished from the kingdom.

"Shock is the only way I can describe it," Dale recalled ruefully. "I knew the new guy would eventually want to bring in his own players, but I thought I could control the situation, the timing, if they decided to ease me out. I didn't want to be told 'Sayonara' on somebody else's schedule.

"It wasn't so much that I didn't get the top job, as I didn't even get to keep my own job. One advantage I had is that I had helped other people go through this experience in our company over the years. So when the other shoe dropped, I told them they didn't have to read me my rights. I already knew the routine by heart."

Drummond had other advantages. His severance package was healthy. The company allowed him extra time on the job to close out projects and prepare for disemployment. And his family and friends were very supportive in his time of need.

Still the whole experience rankled him and caused some introspective moments: "To this day, I maintain an affection for my old employer. They handled the termination with good grace and intelligence. And yet I feel I've been scarred by the experience.

"It's made me think about the bonds of loyalty that used to exist in business organizations and are no longer viable. About the selfish syndrome that permeates both sides of the employer-employee relationship where CYA is the operative strategy for both. The sad part of the whole thing is you no longer have a career, you have a job."

Drummond's advice for still-employed managers: "Manipulate the corporate environment to get experience in a lot of functional areas. Network. Establish lines of communication with different levels in management ranks, especially up the ladder. Figure out the real, not written, organizational system at your firm and learn how to tap it."

And for those who have been let go: "Share the experience with others. The worst thing you can do is hold all your feelings inside. Get help and give help. It makes for a smoother transition."

Drummond's happy ending includes a new job in which he "looks forward to getting to the office every day." Greater utilization of his diverse skills. A larger paycheck. No change in his chosen lifestyle. And a new perspective on helping other managers to help themselves when caught in the crunch of a job loss.

Note: One other big advantage Dale Drummond had was his wife, Linda. He credits her with tremendous understanding and support during the entire affair.

"I think I was angrier than Dale when the ax fell," Linda asserted. "The whole situation seemed topsy-turvy. I just couldn't understand the insensitivity of the firing.

"Dale is a combination of head and heart, and I don't see much room for that kind of man in the cold corporation of today. More's the pity. But that combination is the very reason I admire and love him.

"I've seen a lot of this sort of thing (firing) and the feelings generated by it. Panic. Shame. Depression. As a family, we never felt he let us down or anything like that. And we let him know that. In fact, I truly feel that through pain comes growth. And while no one would consciously opt for this kind of pain, I firmly believe that *we are both better off for this experience.*"

OLD SEEDS GROW INTO NEW JOB

Elmer Norton had spent more than two and a half decades at one firm, and he had risen to a top post that dealt with the public as its main audience. But his company, like many major organizations on the American business scene, suffered fear and trembling at the prospect of becoming a target for corporate raiders.

So cost cutting and downsizing became the order of

the day in an effort to increase profitability and buttress stock prices against the onslaught of the Wall Streeters. The company offered early retirement incentives, but Norton felt they weren't for him.

The slash-backs continued, as Norton knew they would. His division was hit on a "selective" basis. That is, whomever top management perceived as important got to stay; the rest were ushered out the door. Elmer Norton was one of the latter group.

"My immediate reaction was one of sadness, disappointment, and discouragement," said Norton. "I knew that at my age, no corporation was going to come after me. While I had a very strong feeling that I should keep going and keep climbing, I felt that it was unrealistic to expect to get back into the corporate world where I'd spent my entire working life. And I wasn't sure I wanted to."

While still working, in conjunction with his normal activities, Norton discovered that there was a great need in the public sector for the kind of expertise he and his subordinates could offer. He created a joint project that his company approved, something that he really believed in. That project got very good results. He then went to a business association to involve it, so that this idea could be spread all over the state. At about that time he was severed. He said, however, that because of that project, "the last few years were the most enjoyable and most fruitful of my entire career."

Norton had little to do during the first six months after discharge. He did have colleagues call him and ask for help on certain projects, and he helped. But that wasn't what he really wanted to do.

"I'm a physical person," Norton noted, "not in the sense of athletics, but doing physical things. So I decided to build myself an office in my house, to build my own desk, to move walls and do physical things like that. Those things are time consuming and rewarding because I was building something on my own. That kept me going.

"What I had in mind to do from that office was to pursue foundation money and other funding people so that I could continue the type of work that the previous project had involved. Meantime, the association had made a proposal to Washington to get a grant to continue the project that we'd started while I was still employed. It got a large sum of money, which was surprising considering the deficit in these times. The Washington guy actually came to our state to institute the funding."

Association officials then called Norton and asked him to get involved again as a consultant. He's not on the payroll but prefers it that way. It's not only enjoyable and fruitful but keeps him very busy. "I've never been happier with what I've been doing than I am now.

"I feel sorry for those who have no plans when they've been let go," Norton said. "What I've got is a harvest from seeds sown some years before, but seeds sown without the intent of it turning into something else. What I think happens is that if you really *believe in what you're doing,* as I did those last years at my old company, then you'll do okay no matter what happens, if you continue to believe."

As for overcoming his discouragement after the job loss, Norton said, "I discussed the whole situation very carefully with my wife. She's a very strong person. She has made me a much stronger person. You have to have someone like that for support. Actually, I have to take you back to an incident that happened quite a few years ago. It was while I was at my former firm, and I had a terrible siege of depression that was work related.

"One Sunday morning, my wife said 'Get up, we're going for a walk.' It was a terrible, rainy day out, but she made me go. It was like a forced march, and we walked a very long time. By its end, that was a turning point for me. I got over my depression. I have never forgotten that experience and think of it when I need help."

Norton waxed philosophical: "You must look at the situation you're in and not let it beat you down. You must recognize that you just do not give up. You can't be cynical and discouraged. It's just one life you have to live and it's worth living. When situations arise, you have to tackle them with some help. Go out and take part in it—in life.

"I learned in industry that the greatest resource in this country is the individual human being. If that resource is not given a chance to develop and to be fully and properly utilized, then our country is lost. This country's management needs a tremendous overhaul. It has gotten into the hands of people who only look to the bottom line. The human side of business must come first, not last."

THE WRITE STUFF

Unlike Elmer Norton's disemployment, which was done with a rapier, Neil Dempsey's was accomplished with a sledgehammer. His entire department was deep-sixed, lock, stock, and barrel. The only things left behind were empty desks and former colleagues wondering where it would all end.

Dempsey's thirty or so years on the job, frequent relocations and numerous awards, bonuses and citations meant nothing. The first word he got from Personnel was "You're on your own—your only job now is to find a new job." No internal job postings. No reference to referrals. No reasons for the termination. Just the old heave-ho.

"It used to be when the company asked you to move, there was a sort of contract. You'd do what they asked, and they'd take care of you. That's all gone now. There are no more 'gentlemen' running corporations today. They don't want to look at facts, only at the numbers. They're all the same."

Dempsey took the option of half-pay until he became eligible for early retirement. He also received outplacement help, which he was completely turned off by. It wasn't the best of times by any means.

"My self-esteem was destroyed. But I saw the same things happening to a lot of others too. It was always some mysterious 'they' who were doing this to us. We were never told who made the decision or the choices in cutting. I hadn't looked for a job for thirty years, for chrissakes. I felt bitter, and I was discouraged, turned off by the idea of having to look for a job."

Dempsey's wife was just as bitter as he was. She railed at the logic of the decision after all those years and all those previous uprootings. She had an extra burden at the time—less than six months earlier she had been operated on for cancer.

Surrounded by friends and family in the same state of shock that he was, Dempsey took a month to get himself organized for his job search. Networking got him an out-of-state job offer, which he rejected. His wife's health and children's schooling tilted his decision in favor of staying put and continuing to look.

He considered starting his own firm, but rejected the notion when he realized the negative impact it would have on his family and the amount of time he could spend with them. While he had an almost overwhelming urge to get back in the work harness, he now demurred.

First he reviewed his financial position. With a very little rearrangement of certain habits, he felt he could easily live on the reduced income at his disposal. After a lot of internal searching, he had made up his mind— he was going to do what he wanted to do, not what someone else wanted him to do, which is what he'd done all his life.

Dempsey was going to grab for his personal brass ring. Like many, he had entertained grandiose ideas about writing the great American novel or becoming the next Ernest Hemingway or Red Smith in his younger days. Now was his chance, and he was determined to seize it. So he did. And he's doing quite nicely, thank you, with enough writing assignments to keep him comfortably busy for as long as he wants. Nevertheless, the bad taste remains from his dismissal.

He feels strongly that what the company did to people like him will come back to haunt it. "They're mortgaging the future," he claimed, "looking for current profits and not protecting the future of the company, the employees or the stockholders. They're trying to fight the war with all lieutenants and no dogfaces."

His advice to managers who may be in job danger: Recognize that there is a new corporate mindset. The people who did the original hiring in the old days are gone. The new people have different attitudes, and you're in imminent danger of being blind-sided. You can't trust the people at the top. You must look out for yourself.

"The guy with twenty-five years at a company is in a very awkward position," said Dempsey. "Companies don't want to pay for experience anymore. They're now content to do with less-experienced and cheaper people. They think it's okay to hire people whose knowledge comes from textbooks, the Harvard and Wharton MBAs.

"Years ago, many of the top managers hadn't even been to college. But as time went by, they began to put in rules that everyone must have a college education. And other rules. How many companies today would hire a Steinmetz or Edison? One was a hunchback and the other used a hearing aid."

His advice to those who suffer dislocation: Look at a pink slip as an opportunity. It's hard to do. But this is the chance to do what you really want. Ask yourself if you'll really be happy going back to doing what you've been doing all along. Think about that.

"Working the same job can get to be like a habit, like smoking. Look at your hobbies, your interests, your dreams. This may be the chance to make a switch. Study your options. Maybe *it's time to do something for yourself*, as long as it doesn't hurt your family."

Neil Dempsey seized his chance. He admitted that the money isn't as good, but said with a satisfied smile: "I'm having a lot more fun. I feel a lot closer to my wife and kids. And it's funny, but I'm even busier now than I was then. I wouldn't trade my decision for anything."

NEW TWIST, SAME STORY

Rick Charles's story has a peculiar twist to it. He wasn't exactly fired. More like a mutual parting of the ways. But he went through many of the same emotions and harbored many of the same doubts that other managers do when a job shift becomes imminent.

Lured from a job and a region he was fairly happy in, Charles found his new position "a bad fit." "I was frustrated and upset," admitted Charles. "I wondered what I had done to deserve such a bad hand in life. I hated it. The company had lied; the job wasn't what was promised. I had to get back to something I liked."

After much internal anguish accompanied by an unhealthy dose of depression, Charles decided he had to make a move, if only to keep himself marketable, much less sane.

"I couldn't keep my feelings submerged, and that affected my work negatively," said Charles. "The company recognized it, I recognized it. It was time to move. But along with my frustration and anger, I was afraid. I didn't know what was out there. I didn't know how to go about marketing myself, which was ironic since I was in marketing."

Unlike Dempsey, Charles found outplacement a boon, not a bane. The process helped him conduct a disciplined, methodical campaign, much like marketing campaigns he had run in the past. Only now *he* was the product.

"The entire outplacement process is valuable in and of itself," he said. "It teaches you to be proactive. Helps you target your own specific audiences. Gives what-if scenarios to help make decisions. Offers experienced advice. Most of all, I now feel that I control my own destiny. And I appreciate the value of helping people. That feeling can't be underestimated."

At first, "everyone is interested but no one's putting an offer on the table." But then Charles got several offers in rapid-fire succession and took one that made him a vice-president in the field of his choice and back in the region of the country where he wanted to be.

"There was a lot of mental anguish before I took this job," said Charles. "But it complements all the experiences I've had, and it's a great long-term setup. While it doesn't have the prestigious name and deep-pockets resources that came with the last job, I feel very good about taking it. It looks perfect."

NEW YEAR'S EVE RESOLUTION

Termination troubles don't discriminate by race, age— or sex. Margaret Malloy found that out the hard way. Like Rick Charles, she had been enticed from a comfortable position at a major firm by a bucket of promises.

The added fillip that made the promises so promising was that they were made by a close personal friend.

How could she go wrong? The strong implications from her pal were that she would be able to flex her entrepreneurial muscles and eventually assume the mantle of chief operating officer of a dynamic and exciting organization.

Six months later she was fired.

"We had irreconcilable differences, you know, like they say in divorce cases," said Malloy sardonically. "The way I wanted to get things done and the way the guy who hired me wanted to get things done were worlds apart. The only thing we agreed on was the fact that we disagreed—on almost everything."

So how does a veteran manager with years of experience handling tough business situations react?

"It was the most devastating thing that ever happened to me in my entire life, period," Malloy admitted. "During the first six months after I was fired, I had a hard time going on interviews without being on the verge of tears. I was a wreck.

"My biggest mistake was that I took it personally. I saw it as a personal failure. When I look back on it now, I realize I shouldn't have felt that way. But I look around and see many people today feeling the same feelings and making the same mistake.

"I think if individuals to whom this happens can put their own situations into perspective, things would be different. They'd see the same thing is happening to many other qualified, competent, and intelligent people. When viewed that way, termination is just a slight detour, and it's much easier to get back on track."

Malloy didn't exactly take her own advice. It was almost half a year before she was able to "get up, get going, and turn it around." She points to a New Year's Eve conversation she had with herself.

"It may sound weird, but I sat there and looked at my own situation and I said to myself: 'Hey, things aren't so bad. You're fortunate to have all the things you have.

Don't be stupid. Everything is going to be all right.' And eventually it was."

Malloy did a few other things besides talk to herself to weather the aftermath of the crushing blow of her first and only career pink slip. For one, she raised up her usual physical fitness program an extra notch, making it more rigorous than usual. She recognized that physical activity helps immensely during mental depression. For another, she did a lot of volunteer work, exercising her business skills to help an organization that sorely needed her. In fact, she was further buoyed by a job offer from that volunteer group, although she declined it.

Malloy also received an unexpected boost from a mystery source shortly after she had been canned. A total stranger called to say that he had heard of her business prowess and that he had a short-term proposition for her. He wanted Malloy to run his manufacturing firm for several weeks while he made a business trip out of the country.

"Here was someone asking me to take over all his assets and care for them," she said, "and he didn't even know me. I accepted and the job kept me busy, helped put the firing out of my mind, and dropped a few dollars in my pocket. It helped a lot. Both that offer and the volunteer one helped me get through some really bad times."

Now those bad times are over. Malloy was eventually offered several opportunities and was able to pick and choose the one she really wanted.

"When I finally decided, it was terrific. I was delighted. I'm sure it was the right one for me. In the long run, *this is a far better job than the one I was fired from.* It's financially better. I bring more to the party. And it's a better fit. Plus, one of the most reaffirming things is that the people in the new organization tell me I'm doing a good job. I couldn't be happier."

TERMINATION ROLE REVERSAL

"I absolutely couldn't believe my ears when the boss told me I was gone," claimed Don Clements. "They repeatedly—and I mean repeatedly—told me how good a job I was doing. How valuable I was to the firm. Told me that stuff without me ever asking.

"I gotta admit, I felt sorrier for the boss than for me. He was taking it worse than I was. It was a real downer for him. Shortest session we ever had together. Ended up, I told him I felt sorry for him."

But Clements could be forgiven for feeling a little sorry for himself too. After twenty-seven years on the job, he was well paid and highly respected, enjoying the fruits of a long and strong employer-employee relationship. Now the taste had turned sour. He was never given a reason for the dismissal. Just told "strictly a business move."

"I guess I still have some bad feelings toward some people," said Clements, "although I really felt sorry for my boss when I went in to clean out my office. And they did provide me with another little office to carry on my search. So I never really let anger get the best of me and I kept up all my contacts on the job."

Anger did get the best of some of his friends. "I can't begin to tell you how many phone calls I got the first weekend," Clements chuckled. "Many of my pals were so mad, I ended up counseling them."

Clements post-termination activity began with a session with a behavioral scientist followed by eighteen holes of golf with his "Rock of Gibraltar" wife. He fielded dozens of solicitous phone calls but the reality of the situation didn't hit him until he sat down and tried to figure out just what he was going to do with his derailed business career.

"I wanted to make an intelligent decision, based on what I wanted, not what someone offered," Clements maintained. "I asked myself 'Where do I want to go from here?' My main concern became finding something I would be happy doing. And my wife served as my crutch, propping me up, encouraging me to pass up anything I thought wasn't exactly right."

After rejecting a number of early nibbles on his job search line, Clements ran into a dry spell and began to question his strategy. But he got lucky with a consulting project and was kept busy and productive for a short period.

Then the big bite came. He found a business he wanted to buy and after strenuous negotiations, the deal was set. He drove to the final meeting, cleared up some loose ends, and shook hands on the "done deed." Only the deal became undone as he drove home. One of the sellers got cold feet, and suddenly Clements felt "even worse than when I got dumped from my job." This one really hurt the most.

"I had made the decision and I got shot down," remembered Clements. "I felt awful. But within one week, I had four new offers, including one from my original company, which wanted me back in a new capacity. I was walking on air. From the depths to the heights in one fell swoop."

Clements eventually took a job that offered him "total control" of a major segment of the firm. He received "incredible" support from top management, and has gained complete confidence in the correctness of his decision.

"It's just tremendous, better than I ever expected," Clements enthused. "I've made some good decisions, and they've been recognized by my superiors. In fact, my boss said to me 'Where were you twenty years ago? Where have you been all my life?' Nothing could make me feel better.

"And you know what? I learned a lot from this experience. I'm a hell of a lot better person. I'm more understanding, more fair in my dealings with people, especially subordinates. I don't jump to conclusions anymore. I think I'm a better manager.

"Oh, and one other thing. For the last fifteen years at my former job, I must have received hundreds, maybe thousands, of résumés. I didn't read one. Now I read every single one I get. I feel like I'm doing something. It helps me."

BACK TO THE FUTURE

Since the first pages of this book began with the saga of Jack Kable, it seems appropriate that the last pages close with it.

It took about a month after discharge for Jack to get himself into the kind of mental condition that he would need to present himself properly to a prospective employer. He says that he wanted to start the job search sooner rather than later, but instead took his outplacement counselor's advice that he needed some time for preparation and to get over the initial, very common, and to-be-expected "down" feelings. "You can't seek a job until you're ready to sell yourself," he said.

Jack did have an extra, somewhat unique separation benefit allowed him by his former boss. He was able to arrange with his former secretary (with the boss's approval) to have her answer with his name incoming calls on her direct line at the office. Then she would use the telephone's call-forwarding feature to transfer the call to his home telephone.

That benefit gave him at least two advantages: (1) in the event he did not pick up at home, his former secretary would take messages, and (2) it gave callers the initial impression that he was still employed, since he could include his old office number on his résumés and letters (for reasons unknown, employed individuals are much more desirable candidates in the eyes of headhunters and potential employers than those "on the beach").

What steps did Jack follow to land a new job? Many of those techniques recommended in earlier chapters for one. He listed all the people he knew, winnowing the list of those who were most likely to help. He called the best for lunch on the basis that he "would like to talk over my situation and to get your advice." He answered ads in *The Wall Street Journal* and *The New York Times*. He contacted executive search firms and got into their files.

When he made a contact, such as during a luncheon engagement, he always asked for the name of another person from whom he might seek advice, always avoiding the pressure on the individual of seeking a yes or no as to the possibilities of a job offer from that specific person. "That way it relieves the pressure on you, too," said Jack, "as well as any pressure on the person you're meeting with."

The upshot: In four months Jack had a job offer from a very large concern in an entirely different industry, though a position that fully utilized his previous experience and educational background. His new base salary came in at about 5 percent under his former employer's base salary. The annual bonus, however, substantially exceeded his previous one. Overall, the pay package not only beat his previous employer's for the first year, but gave him an opportunity within the first few years to increase his gross pay by at least 50 percent—possibly more. Fringe benefits in every area were at least equal to those he'd received from the company that he had faithfully served for the previous seventeen years.

The source of his new job? "Networking, networking, and more networking," said Jack. A friend and neighbor who worked for Jack's new employer sent his résumé to the head of a division of the firm which he knew was seeking new staff. Almost simultaneously, the outplacement consultant who had been working with Jack had the same thought that the new firm could use someone with Jack's background. He, too, sent a résumé. As Jack said, "The executive at the new firm called me and said, 'I've had two of your résumés land on my desk nearly the same day coming from two different people, both of whom I respect. I think we should meet.'" They did, and Jack was shortly thereafter made an offer, which he accepted.

A fluke, you say? Simply coincidence that wouldn't happen one time in a million? Just luck? Not really. If you work at networking, follow every avenue open to you, set achievement goals, and work hard to reach them, you will always make things happen. Luck occurs when preparation and opportunity meet.

How does Jack feel today about the trials he went through? "I feel I've benefited in some ways from going through all that's happened to me. I must admit that's easy to say now that I've got a job. It's only been a couple months since I began, and I'm still feeling new. I continue to have some apprehension. From now on I'm going to be more externally oriented, more involved with people on the outside as well as with those within. I'm going to be networking for the rest of my life. But I do like my new position and I'm doing well. *I feel whole again.*"